Brideshead Revisited

A play

Roger Parsley

Adapted from the novel by
Evelyn Waugh

Samuel French — London
New York - Toronto - Hollywood

ISBN 0 573 01730 1

Please see page iv for further copyright information

Brideshead Revisited by Evelyn Waugh was originally
published by Methuen Ltd

The extract from "The Waste Land" by T. S. Eliot is reproduced
by permission of Faber and Faber Ltd

BRIDESHEAD REVISITED

First presented by the SNAP Theatre Company at the Gordon Craig Theatre, Stevenage on 3rd February, 1993, with the following cast:

Charles Ryder	Andrew Loudon
Sebastian Flyte	David Willoughby
Julia Flyte	Lisa Turner
Cordelia/Effie/Celia	Miranda Moss
Hooper/Mulcaster/Brideshead	Brian Orrell
Nanny/Lady Marchmain/Cara	Shirley Hafey
Blanche/Mr Ryder/Lord Marchmain	Barney Long
Aloysius	Laurence

Directed by Andy Graham
Designed by Mark Viner
Choreographed by Josette Bushell-Mingo
Music composed by Stuart De La Mere

ACT I

1943

SCENE 1	The grounds at Brideshead

1923

SCENE 2	Mr Ryder's house
SCENE 3	Charles's rooms at Oxford
SCENE 4	Sebastian's rooms at Oxford
SCENE 5	Near Brideshead
SCENE 6	Brideshead
SCENE 7	Charles's rooms at Oxford
SCENE 8	Mr Ryder's house
SCENE 9	Brideshead
SCENE 10	Brideshead
SCENE 11	The roof of Brideshead Castle
SCENE 12	Venice
SCENE 13	Charles's rooms at Oxford
SCENE 14	London
SCENE 15	Brideshead
SCENE 16	Sebastian's rooms at Oxford
SCENE 17	Mr Ryder's house

ACT II

SCENE 1	Brideshead
SCENE 2	Brideshead
SCENE 3	Charles's Paris studio
SCENE 4	Brideshead
SCENE 5	Sebastian's house in Fez
SCENE 6	Marchmain House, London

Years later

SCENE 7	An ocean liner
SCENE 8	An art exhibition
SCENE 9	Brideshead
SCENE 10	Mr Ryder's house
SCENE 11	Brideshead
SCENE 12	Brideshead
SCENE 13	Brideshead

1943

SCENE 14	The grounds at Brideshead

CHARACTERS

Charles Ryder
Sebastian Flyte
Julia Flyte
Cordelia Flyte
Brideshead Flyte
Boy Mulcaster
Anthony Blanche
Mr Ryder, Charles's father
Lady Marchmain
Lord Marchmain
Cara, Lord Marchmain's lover
Celia Ryder, Charles's wife
Rex Mottram, Julia's fiancé
Hooper, a soldier
Ma Mayfield
Effie
Jasper, Charles's cousin
Nanny Hawkins
Mr Samgrass
Kurt
Father Phipps
Policeman
Aloysius, Sebastian's teddy bear

The action takes place in 1943 and in flashback to twenty
years earlier

AUTHOR'S NOTE

As this play consists largely of a journey into the past by the central character, Charles Ryder, it is suggested that in production a dream-like quality be explored, especially in the inter-scene sequences: sometimes giving the effect of shadows moving, at others the feeling that one scene has simply slipped easily into another. The setting has thus to be as flexible as possible — using drapes, levels, screens, moveable flats, etc. However, the stage directions and scenic indications should be taken as starting points or suggestions only — the director and company should find their own way. In the original production, music was specially composed to support the style employed, but of course, there are many ways of approaching this aspect, too; some of the works of Thomas Tallis and/or Edward Elgar might be found useful.

In the original production there was a cast of seven (M4, F3). The characters have been grouped below to show how the necessary doubling was achieved, but the play could obviously be performed by a cast of anything up to 22 (M14, F8).

M1: **Charles Ryder**
M2: **Sebastian Flyte**
M3: **Hooper/Boy Mulcaster/Jasper/Father Phipps/ Brideshead Flyte/Kurt**
M4: **Mr Ryder//Anthony Blanche/Lord Marchmain/ Rex Mottram/Policeman/Mr Samgrass**

F1: **Julia Flyte**
F2: **Cordelia Flyte/Effie/Celia Ryder**
F3: **Nanny Hawkins/Cara/Ma Mayfield/Lady Marchmain**

For Alison

ACT I
SCENE 1

The grounds of Brideshead Castle. 1943

Music. As the house lights go down, we become aware of the sound of lorries passing, and we see the sweep of their headlamps

We can also see Charles Ryder, standing with a clipboard in his hand. As the sound of the lorries fades, a Light comes up behind a gauze showing us the Flyte family as if in a photograph. Charles smiles wryly. This image then fades, and the Lights change to a representation of early dawn. The music fades as Charles speaks

Charles Hooper! Hooper! Where the hell are you?

Hooper enters, doing up the buttons of his greatcoat. He too, has a clipboard

Hooper Sorry. Call of nature, I'm afraid. Couldn't be helped. Right. Better make a start, I suppose. (*He examines the notes on his clipboard with the aid of a torch*)

Charles You should have started half an hour ago. It should all be ready for checking by now.

Hooper Ah, yes. Well, you see I had a bit of a rush getting my gear together this morning — you know how it is. It was pretty dark last night when we got here. Things got a bit ... mislaid.

Charles How you ever managed in business I'll never know, Hooper.

Hooper Well, it's different in business.

Charles Yes. It must be.

Hooper Looks like a decent place, this time.

Charles What?

Hooper Decent billet.

Charles Is it?

Hooper I've been looking round. It's just sort of parkland here, of course, could be anywhere. But beyond those trees there's a big house. We'd better check it over, later. Massive grounds.

Charles Where are we? Do you know yet?

Hooper South. Must be south; the train took all day. Anywhere better than Glasgow, though. Next to that lunatic asylum. You know, I really thought we were going to have a go at Hitler, get an overseas posting, this time, didn't you? All this waiting. Still, as I say, this looks like being decent.

Charles Good.

Hooper You've been in since the start, haven't you?

Charles Three and a half years. We were all volunteers at the beginning. Special Reserve unit. Started, trained together. Then the delays, the postings here and there. Never any action. One way and another the originals have nearly all gone. You know, Hooper ... all this waiting has aged me.

Hooper It's the enthusiasm that goes, isn't it?

Charles I was in love at one time.

Hooper In love?

Charles With the army — with the idea of doing something ... something positive; making a statement about life ... about my life. There was reason ... a cause — a calling. I must say the voice is very faint now.

Hooper Still, better just to get on with it. (*Pause*) You know, there's something a bit odd about this place.

Charles Odd?

Hooper Well, it's called a castle — at least, there's a sign saying so down at what I suppose must be the main gate — but there are no battlements or towers or anything. Just a sort of dome on top. Now why's that, I wonder?

Charles A dome? What's the name? The name on the gate?

Hooper Brideshead.

Music

Yes ... that was it. Brideshead Castle. Have you heard of it?

Charles (*distantly*) Brideshead ...

Hooper Means something to you, does it?

Charles It was part of my life. Perhaps the whole of my life. It's called Brideshead because there's a stream — The Bride. Rises a couple of miles away at a farm called "Bridesprings". It's dammed below the house to make three lakes.

Hooper That's right. There is some water down there.

Charles (*slowly; shaking his head*) Do you know, this place was planned one hundred and fifty years ago — the house, the trees, the parkland — to have reached its maturity now? Now, when it's crawling with billeted corporals, no doubt casting their cigarette stubs into the fountain!

Hooper If you've been here before you're in for a bit of a shock, I should imagine. Must have been some place. Round the front they've put up tents and huts and a lorry turn-round, and there's a new tarmac road driven through the trees. It's a bit of a mess — from the outside, anyway. And there's a queer thing, too — there's a sort of Catholic Church attached to the house. I looked in ... there was some kind of service going on. Just a padre and one old lady.

Charles (*to himself*) The chapel ...

Hooper Did you say you'd been here? Is that how you know about it?

Charles Yes ... I've been here ... I know all about it ...

Music

Twenty years ago, it must be ... twenty years ...

The Lights fade on Hooper and he exits

Charles begins to take off his army greatcoat under which he has his undergraduate clothes

At the same time, the Lights come up behind the gauze to reveal Charles's father

SCENE 2

Mr Ryder's house. 1923

Mr Ryder Charles ... Charles!

Charles Father? Sorry. Just changing.

Mr Ryder We need to speak ...

Charles Yes, well actually I wanted to ask you something, too. Won't be a second.

Mr Ryder I've been talking about you — I happened to meet your future warden at the Athenaeum. I wanted to talk about the Etruscan notions of immortality; he wanted to talk about extension lectures for the working-class; so we compromised and talked about you. I asked him what your allowance should be.

Charles Ah well, actually that's what I wanted to ——

Mr Ryder He said, "Three hundred a year; that's all most men have." I thought that a deplorable answer. I had more than most men when I was up. I toyed with the idea of giving you six hundred, but I reflected that, should the warden come to hear of it, it might sound deliberately impolite. So I shall give you five hundred and fifty.

Charles Thank you very much.

Mr Ryder Yes, it's indulgent of me, but it all comes out of capital, you know. Well, anyway, that's what I wanted to tell you. I only wish I had some words of wisdom for you, but ... I haven't. Your cousin Jasper has been at Oxford for two years, as you know.

Charles Thank you.

Mr Ryder He tells me you will have ground floor rooms.

Charles Yes, I believe so.

Mr Ryder I should change them. People start dropping in. They leave their gowns there and come and collect them before hall; you start giving them sherry. Before you know where you are, you've opened a free bar for all the undesirables in the college. Well, good luck, Charles.

He exits

SCENE 3

Charles's rooms at Oxford. Night

Music. The gauze lifts, the Lights change, and Charles walks into his university room, sits and begins reading. There is the sound of approaching male laughter. A bell tolls

Mulcaster staggers on

Sebastian (*off*) Here, hold up, Mulcaster, old thing. I'm about done ...

Mulcaster Come on, or we'll never make it.

Sebastian staggers on holding his teddy bear, Aloysius

Sebastian Plenty of time. Don't have to be in House till Tom stops ringing. Feeling a bit wobbly down below — must go steady. Aloysius is anxious that I don't make an exhibition of myself: you see his look of disapprobation?

Mulcaster All right. Steady, by all means. But at least move.

Sebastian Do you know, I feel most uncommonly unwell. Here. (*He gives Aloysius to Mulcaster*) I don't think Aloysius should see this. I must leave you a minute ... (*He is sick into Charles's window*)

Mulcaster Oh, you ass, Flyte! You might have chosen the flower-beds! Well, at least you'll travel lighter. Come on. (*He puts his arm around Sebastian and begins to move him off*)

Charles comes to the window. Mulcaster turns and comes back to him. Sebastian stares at Charles

Terribly sorry, old chap. The wines were too various. It was neither the quality nor the quantity that was at fault. It was the mixture. Grasp that, and you have the root of the matter. To understand all is to forgive all. (*He starts to stagger off towards Sebastian*)

Sebastian returns to the window, looking intensely at Charles. He hands him a card

Sebastian That's where I am, and who I am: do come and see me tomorrow. Please?

Mulcaster Come on!

Sebastian (*taking Aloysius from Mulcaster*) Come on, Aloysius. It's all right. All over, now ...

Sebastian and Mulcaster stagger out

SCENE 4

Sebastian's rooms at Oxford

Music. The Lights cross-fade as Charles walks towards Sebastian's room

Sebastian enters

Sebastian Ah! Come in, come in.

Charles walks in

I knew you'd come. Aloysius thought you wouldn't. Sorry about last night.
Am I forgiven?

Charles Yes, of course.

Sebastian Thank you. Charles, isn't it? I found out! We're having
plovers' eggs. Mummy sends them from Brideshead. They always lay
early for her. I'm hoping Blanche may drop in, too — do you know
him? That means that there are five each and two over, so I'm having
the two. I'm unaccountably hungry today. Ah, Blanche!

Anthony Blanche enters

Come on, we've got plovers' eggs!

Blanche My dear, I'm afraid that I shall be unable to do justice to them.
I've been lunching with my p-p-preposterous tutor. He thought it very
odd my leaving when I did. I told him I had to change for f-f-footer.

Sebastian This is Charles Ryder. We met ignobly, but I am forgiven.
Ryder — Anthony Blanche.

Charles Hallo.

Blanche Hallo, dear one. (*To Sebastian*) How absolutely charming! (*He
glances through the window*) Oh my dears, my dears! Rowists! All
sweatered and muffled on their way to the river! I must speak to them.
(*He grabs a megaphone and stands on the window-ledge*)
"I, Tiresias, have foresuffered all
Enacted on this same d-divan or b-bed.
I, who have sat by Thebes below the wall,
And walked among the l-l-lowest of the dead!"
(*He steps back into the room*) How I surprised them! All boatmen are Grace
Darlings to me! Do you know, I really think a walk by the river would lift
the spirit somewhat. Do you mind?

Sebastian (*laughing*) Of course not. Have fun!

Blanche Oh I will, I will! My dear. (*He embraces Sebastian*) I should like
to stick you full of barbed arrows, like a p-pin-cushion. (*He turns to
Ryder*) And where do you lurk?

Charles Ground floor, front quad.

The next line is said with particular meaning and shared looks with Sebastian

Sebastian has already found it!

Blanche Intrigue, intrigue! I shall come down your burrow and ch-ch-chivy you out like an old s-s-stoat!

Mulcaster appears at the window, steals Aloysius from a chair and flings him into the room, hitting Sebastian

Sebastian Mulcaster! We'll get you for that!

Music. A students' mêlée begins, with a chase ending in a rugby scrum, during which Charles and Sebastian sit on Mulcaster and pull his trousers down. During some of this horseplay, there is a moment, held for a couple of seconds, where Charles and Sebastian are holding each other, and look deeply into each other's eyes — they are in love. Blanche, very much on the fringe of things, sees this with some jealousy registering in his face. Finally, Mulcaster, Charles, and Sebastian are left lying about, exhausted

Blanche Well, what fun and games! No-one else for a riverside stroll?

They indicate not

Well, then ... (*He turns to Charles*) I think it's perfectly brilliant of Sebastian to have discovered you! Farewell, farewell.

He exits

A clock chime is heard

Mulcaster Oh, Christ! I've got a lecture!

He exits awkwardly, pulling up his trousers

Charles and Sebastian laugh at him

Charles Oh!
Sebastian What?
Charles I've got one, too!

They laugh again, then the mood changes

Sebastian Must you go?

Charles Well, I ought to.

Sebastian Don't go, Charles. Come with me.

Charles Where?

Sebastian I've got a motor-car and a basket of strawberries and a bottle of Château Peyraguey — which isn't a wine you've ever tasted, so don't pretend — it's heaven with strawberries. Will you come?

Charles What, now?

Sebastian Yes, now ...

Again they share that look

Charles Where are we going?

Sebastian To see a friend.

Charles Who?

Sebastian Name of Hawkins. Oh — the motor-car is Hardcastle's. Better return the bits to him if I kill myself — I'm not very good at driving. Hardcastle's in my college. Leads a double life. At least, I assume he does. He couldn't go on being Hardcastle, day and night, always, could he? Or he'd die of it. He says he knows my father, which is impossible.

Charles Why?

Sebastian No-one knows Papa. He's a social leper. Hadn't you heard? Don't sit there looking like a dummy! Come on!

Sebastian grabs Charles's hand and they exit running

Music as the Lights change to:

SCENE 5

Near Brideshead

A green cloth is spread over a raised area of the stage

Sebastian and Charles enter immediately and fling themselves down on to the "bank". Charles turns to Sebastian. They smile at each other, then both lie back

Charles Oh ... this is blissful! Summer scents everywhere ... strawberries, wine ... the sun ... it's as if the very air has been touched by heaven!

I feel as if I've been lifted a finger's breadth above the turf, and held suspended ...

Sebastian Just the place to bury a crock of gold. I should like to bury something precious in every place where I've been happy, and then, when I was old and ugly and miserable, I could come and dig it up and remember. (*Pause*) Sit up. I'll show you something. (*He points*) You see? The woodland that curves around the hill over there? You can just see the dome above the trees ... and some of the house ...

Charles Is that ... Brideshead?

Sebastian (*nodding*) Well?

Charles What a place to live in!

Sebastian You must see the garden front and the fountain. It's where my family live.

Charles Where your family live?

Sebastian Yes, but don't worry. They're in London. (*Pause. He looks at Charles*) You do want to see it, don't you?

Charles Oh, yes — I do, I do ...

Sebastian Come on, then!

He again takes Charles by the hand and drags him off

Music. The Lights cross-fade quickly to:

SCENE 6

Brideshead

Sebastian and Charles come straight back on

Sebastian Everything's shut up. This way. I want you to meet Nanny Hawkins. That's what we've come for. She lives right up in the dome ... (*He indicates that they should be quiet as they step into the room*)

Nanny Hawkins is sleeping, hands lying open, a rosary in her lap

(*He calls softly*) Nanny! Nanny Hawkins!

Nanny (*waking*) Well, this is a surprise.

Sebastian kisses her

Who's this? I don't think I know him.

Sebastian A friend from Oxford, Nanny. Charles Ryder.

Charles Pleased to meet you.

Nanny How do you do. You've come just the right time. Julia's here for the day. Such a time they're all having — the whole family! It'll be October before we're settled down again. It's dull without them. Father Phipps was here on Thursday and I said exactly the same to him.

Sebastian D'you say Julia's here?

Nanny Yes, dear. You must have just missed her. It's the Conservative Women. Her Ladyship was to have done them, but she's poorly. Julia won't be long: she's leaving immediately after her speech, before the tea.

Sebastian I'm afraid we may miss her again.

Nanny Don't do that, dear: it'll be such a surprise to her seeing you — though she ought to wait for the tea. I told her, it's what the Conservative Women come for. Now, what's the news? Are you studying hard at your books?

Sebastian Not very, I'm afraid, Nanny.

Nanny Ah, cricketing all day long, I expect, like your brother. He found time to study, too, though. He's not been here since Christmas, but he'll be back for the Agricultural, I expect. Did you see this piece about Julia in the paper? She brought it down for me ... (*Reading*) "The lovely daughter whom Lady Marchmain is bringing out this season ... witty as well as ornamental ..." Well that's no more than the truth, though it was a shame to cut her hair. I said to Father Phipps, "It's not natural." He said, "Nuns do it", and I said, "Well surely, Father, you aren't going to make a nun out of Lady Julia?" The very idea! Ring the bell, dear, and we'll have some tea.

Sebastian Oh, we can't stop. Sorry, Nanny. Have to get back to Oxford, you see ...

Nanny And miss Julia? She will be upset when she hears. It would have been such a surprise for her. Ah, well ...

Sebastian kisses her

Will you come again before the holidays?

Sebastian I don't know, Nanny.

Nanny Well, it was nice to see you. Now you look after yourself and don't forget your studies.

Sebastian I won't, Nanny.
Nanny Goodbye, Mr Ryder.
Charles Goodbye.

They come out of the room

The Lights fade on Nanny and she exits

Sebastian Poor Nanny. She does have such a dull life. I've a good mind
to bring her to Oxford to live with me, only she'd always be trying to
send me to church.
Charles Sebastian —
Sebastian We must go quickly before my sister gets back.
Charles (*stopping him*) Which are you ashamed of, her or me?

Pause

Sebastian (*looking at Charles*) I'm ashamed of myself. I'm not going to
have you get mixed up with my family. They're so madly charming.
Oh, Charles — all my life they've been taking things away from me.
If they once got hold of you, they'd make you their friend not mine, and
I won't let them.

They exchange glances

Charles All right. But am I not going to be allowed to see any more of
the house?
Sebastian It's all shut up. We came to see Nanny. On Queen Alexandra's
day it's all open for a shilling. (*A slight pause*) Oh, well ... come and
look if you want to. It's only corridors and rooms, really. But there's
the chapel. You must see that.

Organ music plays as the Lights change

*They enter the chapel. Sebastian dips his fingers in the stoup, crosses himself
and genuflects. Charles copies him*

Why did you do that?
Charles Just good manners.

Sebastian Well, you needn't on my account. What do you think of our chapel?
Charles It's ... like a monument to art nouveau.
Sebastian It was Papa's present to Mama.

The music ends

Julia enters the chapel

Sebastian pulls Charles into a shadow on one side

(*Whispering*) Julia.

They watch as Julia genuflects, crosses herself, then exits

Sebastian emerges from the shadow, followed by Charles

I'm sorry. I haven't been very nice this afternoon. Brideshead often has that effect on me. But I had to take you to see Nanny. Why do you look at me like that?
Charles I don't know ... it's just that you're so very mysterious about your family.
Sebastian I rather hoped that I was mysterious about everything! And anyway you seem so ... inquisitive.
Charles Perhaps I am rather curious about other people's families — you see, it's not a thing I know about. There's only my father and myself.
Sebastian You don't know what you've been saved. There are lots of us. Look them up in Debrett. I say ... it's half-past five. We could get to Godstow in time for dinner, leave the car, and then walk back by the river. Wouldn't that be best? Yes?

He links arms with Charles and leads him off

Come on!

They exit

The Lights cross-fade to:

SCENE 7

Charles's rooms at Oxford

Music. We hear students chanting "We want Blanche", followed by a loud cheer and laughter. The laughter fades

Blanche enters. His hair is wet, as are his pyjamas. He is reading aloud

Blanche "'Tomorrow', Mrs Viveash interrupted him, 'will be as awful as today.'"

Charles enters carrying books and a sketch-pad

Charles Blanche! What's happened to you? You're dripping wet!
Blanche Oh, I've had visitors, Charles.
Charles What?
Blanche Boy Mulcaster and a bunch of rather gaudily dressed students came crying at my window, yelling at the tops of their voices.
Charles Yelling what?
Blanche "We want Blanche!" Such a public declaration! I said, "How people will talk!" But they continued to chant my name. My dear, they quite destroyed my concentration — I was reading *Antic Hay*, it's very good, you know — and their desire for me became so overwhelmingly loud that I had to go out and speak with them ... I said, "Now look here, chaps, I may be inverted, but I'm not insatiable! Why don't you come back one at a time?"
Charles But what did they want?
Blanche To put me in Mercury.
Charles The fountain?
Blanche Yes. They began to move rather purposefully towards me at that point, so I said, "Dear sweet clodhoppers. If you knew anything of sexual psychology you would know that nothing could give me keener pleasure than to be manhandled by you meaty boys. So if you wish to be my partner in joy, come and seize me. If, on the other hand, you simply wish to satisfy some obscure and less easily classified libido and see me bathe, come with me quietly, dear louts, to the fountain." Whereupon I walked to Mercury, stepped in, sat down with as much grace as I could muster, and splashed about a bit. And after a few last

unkind words, they departed in search of other sport. Do you think I
could borrow a towel, dear?

Charles Through there. Help yourself.

Blanche (*indicating the book*) I'm afraid my Huxley's in need of some
resuscitation. Ah, well ...

He exits. Jasper enters

Jasper Charles!

Charles Cousin Jasper!

Jasper I find you in, at last. Are you working?

Charles Just about to make a start. At least, trying.

Jasper Hm. Your father asked me to get in touch with you and I've tried
several times in the last week or two. I have the impression that you're
avoiding me. If that is so, Charles, I can't say I'm surprised. You may
think it none of my business, but I feel a sense of responsibility. I
expected you to make mistakes your first year. We all do. But you, my
dear Charles, whether you realize it or not, have gone straight, hook,
line and sinker, into the very worst set in the university. There's that
chap Sebastian Flyte you seem inseparable from. His brother Brideshead was a sound fellow, but this friend of yours looks very odd to me,
and he gets himself talked about. And then there's Anthony Blanche —
now there's a man there's absolutely no excuse for.

Charles (*loudly; aimed at Blanche next door*) I'm not sure I like him
myself.

Jasper Well, he's always hanging round here. They think just because
they have a lot of money to throw about they can do anything. And
that's another thing. I don't know what allowance your father makes
you, but I don't mind betting you're spending double. In debt up to your
ears, I suspect. And you can't be doing any work; you seem to spend
most of your time drinking. No-one minds a man getting tight once or
twice a term, but I hear you're constantly seen drunk in the middle of
the afternoon. It's a bad lot you're in with, Charles.

Charles I'm sorry, Jasper, but I happen to like them. I also like getting
drunk at luncheon, and, though I haven't yet spent quite double my
allowance, I undoubtedly shall before the end of term. I usually have
a glass of champagne about this time — won't you join me?

Blanche enters with a towel around his neck, and another round his waist

Jasper (*turning and seeing Blanche; looking from one to the other*)
Something will have to be done.

He exits

Blanche What a serious fellow!
Charles My cousin Jasper. I'm not too sure of what is in the Riot Act,
but I think I've just been vouchsafed most of its contents.
Blanche Charles. I want to talk to you.
Charles What about?
Blanche Our friend — Sebastian.
Charles Oh.
Blanche I can see he has completely captivated you, Charles. Well, I'm
not surprised. Of course, you haven't known him as long as I have. I
was at school with him. You wouldn't believe it, but in those days
people used to say he was a little bitch; just a few unkind boys who
knew him well. He never seemed to get into trouble. The rest of us were
constantly being beaten, but never Sebastian. We used to go to mass
together, you know — he spent such a time in the confessional I used
to wonder what he had to say. Perhaps he was just being charming
through the grille! I left under what is called a cloud — harrowing
interview with m'tutor, and so on. My dear, the things he knew about
me, which I thought no-one — except possibly Sebastian — knew.
Never trust mild old men or charming schoolboys, dear. (*He sees
Charles's sketch-pad and picks it up*)
Charles I shall make a note.
Blanche (*looking at the drawings*) These are yours, aren't they? I think
your work exquisite, quite delightful. But do you know the other day
I was speaking to Sebastian about you? I said "Charles is an artist. He
draws like a young Ingres." Well, my dear, Sebastian looked at me in
that charming way of his and said, "Yes, Aloysius draws very prettily,
too, but of course he's rather more modern." So amusing ... one
wonders how he came to be born of such a sinister family. I don't
suppose he'll ever let you meet them. He's far too clever. There's his
brother Brideshead — a learned bigot, his sister Julia, whose photograph is always in the illustrated papers, looking incestuous, another
sister in the schoolroom, whose governess went mad and drowned
herself — I'm sure she's abominable — and Lady Marchmain, elegant
and powerful; and then of course there's her husband, who some time
back was lured to Venice by a dubious actress by the name of Cara ...

with such a background you mustn't blame Sebastian if at times he is
a little insipid, particularly as he isn't very well-endowed in the top
storey.

Charles Now, really, Blanche ——

Blanche Tell me candidly, have you ever heard Sebastian say anything
you have remembered for five minutes? No, his utterances are little
spheres of soapsud, full of rainbow light for a second, then — phut!
Vanished, with nothing left at all.

Charles Why are you doing this?

Blanche (*putting a coat on over the towels*) I only hold the mirror. You
choose to see or you don't. Well, my dear, I've no doubt that you'll tell
Sebastian everything I've said about him. And do you know what his
response will be? He will immediately start talking about that amusing
bear of his! Farewell, sweet youth, farewell.

He exits. At the same time Sebastian enters, opposite, with Aloysius

Sebastian Charles! I feel terribly claustrophobic — I must dine out
today! (*He looks off*) There's Blanche!

Charles Yes, he's just been to see me.

Sebastian I hear he's been in Mercury.

Charles Yes.

Sebastian Poor old Antoine! I've just come from mass at the Old Palace.
I haven't been all this term, and Monseigneur Bell asked me to dinner
twice last week, and I know what that means — Mummy's been writing
to him. So I sat bang in front, where he couldn't help seeing me, and
absolutely shouted the Hail Marys at the end. So that's over. Done
much work?

Charles I haven't even opened a book! I've had Cousin Jasper come to
deliver a moral lecture, Blanche to dry himself out, and now you! Did
you know Blanche at Eton?

Sebastian He was sent down in my first term. I remember seeing him
about. He always has been a noticeable figure.

Charles Did he go to mass with you?

Sebastian I don't think so. Why?

Charles Has he met any of your family?

Sebastian Charles, how very peculiar you're being today. No, I don't
supppose so. Why all this interest?

Charles I just wanted to find out how much truth there was in what he
said.

Sebastian I shouldn't think a word. That's his great charm.
Charles You may think it charming. I think it's devilish. Do you know
he spent the whole time trying to turn me against you, and almost
succeeded?
Sebastian Did he? How silly. Aloysius wouldn't approve of that at all.
Would you, you pompous old bear? Now, what do you say — shall we
dine out?
Charles I really oughtn't to. I'm overdrawn quite a bit as it is.
Sebastian Will your father mind?
Charles I don't know.
Sebastian Will you need to tell him?
Charles Oh, yes. Yes, I'll have to talk to him about it in the holidays ...
(*He turns downstage*)

Sebastian exits

The Lights change to:

SCENE 8

Mr Ryder's house

Charles's father enters, carrying a book

Mr Ryder My dear boy, they never told me you were home. Hayter
brought you the evening paper? There is no news, of course — such a
lot of nonsense. What do you like to drink? You must tell Hayter what
you would like and he will get it in. I never keep any wine now. I am
forbidden it, and no-one comes to see me. But while you are here, you
must have what you like. You are here for long?
Charles I'm not quite sure, Father.
Mr Ryder It's a very long vacation. In my day we used to go on reading
parties. Always in mountainous areas. I really cannot think why Alpine
scenery should be thought conducive to study ...
Charles I thought of putting in some time at an art school — in the life
class.
Mr Ryder In my day there was an institution called a "sketching club".
Mixed sexes, bicycles and, it was popularly thought, free love. You
might try that.

Charles One of the problems is money, Father.

Mr Ryder Oh I shouldn't worry about a thing like that at your age.

Charles You see, I've run short.

Mr Ryder Yes? Well I'm the worst person to come to for advice. I've never been "short" as you so painfully put it. And yet what else could you say? "Hard up"? "Impecunious"? "Distressed"? "In Queer Street"? Let us say you are in Queer Street and leave it at that. Your grandfather once said to me, "Live within your means, but if you do get into difficulties, come to me. Don't go to a moneylender —" No, you mustn't worry over money.

Charles Then what do you suggest I do?

Mr Ryder Your cousin Melchior was imprudent with his investments and got into a very Queer Street. He went to Australia. (*He starts to read his book*)

Charles Father, you surely don't want me to spend the whole vacation here with you?

Mr Ryder What?

Charles Won't you find it rather a bore having me at home for so long?

Mr Ryder I trust I should not betray such an emotion even if I felt it. You are very welcome, my dear boy — stay as long as you find it convenient. And then you will be able to keep me up to date with all the new plays.

Charles Father, as I told you, I haven't the money to spare for theatre-going.

Mr Ryder My dear boy. You must not let money become your master in this way. You should go to the play as part of your education. By the way, I'm afraid I can offer nothing wonderful with regard to dinner. Your Aunt Philippa when she was here gave Mrs Abel ten menus, and they have never been varied. It is remarkable how some people are able to put their opinions in tablets of stone; your aunt had that gift ... it was in her mind to make a home with me, you know. But it didn't do. I got her out in the end. I got her out in the end. Oh ... (*he opens his book and takes out a telegram*) ... this came. It's for you. I've signed for it.

Charles opens it and reads

News?

Charles Father, I've got to leave at once.

Mr Ryder Yes?

Charles A great friend of mine at Oxford. He went home a few days ago.
A terrible accident. I just hope I'm not too late. (*He shows his father the telegram*)
Mr Ryder (*reading aloud*) "Gravely injured. Come at once. Sebastian."
Charles Oh, Father — if ... if he dies, I don't know what I shall do!
Mr Ryder Well. I'm sorry you're upset. But reading this message I
should not say that the accident was as serious as you seem to think —
otherwise it would hardly be signed by the victim himself. Still, of
course, he may well be fully conscious but blind ... or paralysed, with
a broken back. Why is your presence so necessary? You have no
medical knowledge. You are not in holy orders. Do you hope for a
legacy?
Charles (*distressed*) Father! I told you, he is a great friend.
Mr Ryder Ah. A friend. Well, I shall miss you, my dear boy, but don't
hurry back on my account.

Mr Ryder exits

*Charles throws his overcoat over his arm, and the Lights change back to the
Brideshead setting*

SCENE 9

Brideshead

Julia enters

Julia You're Mr Ryder? Come in.
Charles I got here as quickly as I could. How is he?
Julia Sebastian? Oh, he's fine. He'll be in in a minute. Have you had
dinner? (*She takes his coat*)
Charles On the train. What's happened to him?
Julia Didn't he say? I expect he thought you wouldn't come if you knew.
He's cracked a bone in his ankle so small it hasn't a name! But they X-
rayed it yesterday, and told him to keep it up for a month. He's been
making the most enormous fuss. Everyone else has gone. He tried to
make me stay back with him — I expect you know how maddeningly
pathetic he can be. I said, "Surely there must be someone you can get
hold of?" So he agreed to try you, and I promised I'd stay if you failed

him, so you can imagine how popular you are with me. It's ... very noble
of you to come at a moment's notice.

Charles How did he do it?

Julia Believe it or not, playing croquet. He lost his temper and tripped
over a hoop. Not a very honourable scar! You've been here before,
haven't you? Nanny told me. We both thought it very odd of you not
to stay to tea.

Charles That was Sebastian.

Julia You seem to let him boss you about a good deal. You shouldn't.
It's very bad for him.

Sebastian enters in a bath chair

(*To Sebastian*) Well, you're all right now — here's your chum.

Charles I thought you were dying.

Sebastian I thought I was, too. The pain was excruciating! Julia, do you
think if you asked him, Wilcox would give us champagne tonight?

Julia I hate champagne, and Mr Ryder has had dinner. And now I'm
going to leave you boys.

Sebastian Where are you off to?

Julia The nursery. I promised Nanny a game of halma. Good-night, Mr
Ryder, and goodbye — I don't suppose we'll meet tomorrow, I'm
leaving early. I can't tell you how grateful I am for relieving me at the
sick-bed. Oh, Sebastian, if Mr Mottram telephones later, tell Wilcox
I'm not to be disturbed.

She exits

Sebastian I'm not running her affairs for her. This Mottram is a rather
unsuitable Canadian, much older than her, and with a murky past and
a Mrs Champion who seems to go with him and Julia would rather she
didn't — Mummy doesn't approve. There must have been a row —
Julia's very pompous tonight.

Charles I don't think she cares for me.

Sebastian I don't think she cares for anyone, much. But I love her.

Charles She's rather like you — in looks, I mean.

Sebastian But not in character. I wouldn't love anyone with a character
like mine. Oh, by the way, while you're here, will you draw the
fountain? I'll have an easel put up ... I can go quite fast in this. Bet I
could beat you round the room.

Charles Of course you couldn't.
Sebastian Ah, but you've got to hop. Here on this line ... ready, steady, go!

They hop and wheel round the room. There is laughter and music, and their movement brings them into the next scene as the Lights change to:

SCENE 10

Brideshead

Charles takes up a seated position and is at work on a drawing. Sebastian drapes his arms around him in a languorous fashion

Charles Why is this house called a castle?
Sebastian It used to be one until they moved it.
Charles What can you mean?
Sebastian Just that. The family had a castle a mile away. It was pulled down, and a new house was built here in the valley. I'm glad they did, aren't you?
Charles If it was mine, I'd never live anywhere else.
Sebastian But you see, Charles, it isn't mine, just at the moment it is, but usually it's full of ravening beasts. (*He reaches out his hand and holds Charles's arm*) If it could only be like this always — always summer, always alone, the fruit always ripe, and Aloysius in a good temper ...
Charles Do try not to jog me. Is the dome by Inigo Jones, too? It looks later.
Sebastian Oh, Charles, don't be such a tourist! It's pretty! What does it matter when it was built or how long it's been there?
Charles It's the sort of thing I like to know. It matters to me.
Sebastian (*looking at the drawing*) I say! You've got it, you know!
Charles Do you think so?
Sebastian The animals, the vegetation, everything! Is it finished?
Charles Yes. I think so. Shall I give it to your mother?
Sebastian Why? You don't know her.
Charles It seems polite. I'm staying in her house.
Sebastian Give it to Nanny. Here! I know! There's Mummy's box of oil paints indoors. She's given up. Someone told her that you could only appreciate the world by painting it, so she bought them. But she was

hopeless. However bright the colours were in the tubes, by the time
Mummy had mixed them up, they came out a kind of khaki! You could
brighten up the office.

Charles I'm not an interior decorator.

Sebastian Panels. There are panels. Just crying out for an artist. Would
you? And we'll open another case of wine. Charles, there's something
I must ask you.

Charles What?

Sebastian Ought we to be drunk every night?

Charles (*laughing*) Yes, I think so.

Sebastian I think so, too.

They laugh, and embrace each other

Father Phipps enters

Father Phipps Good-day, good-day, gentlemen.

Sebastian (*breaking from Charles*) Good-day, Father.

Father Phipps Surrey in trouble, I'm afraid.

Sebastian What?

Father Phipps Middlesex have them in their sights, don't you think?

Sebastian Oh ... cricket. Charles and I don't know much about it.

Father Phipps I wish I'd seen Tennyson make that fifty-eight last
Thursday. That must have been an innings! The account in *The Times*
was excellent. Did you see him against the South Africans?

Charles I'm afraid ... I've never seen him.

Father Phipps Neither have I. I haven't seen a first-class match for
years. After we'd been to the induction of the Abbot at Ampleforth,
Father Graves looked up a train which gave us three hours to wait on
the afternoon of the match with Lancashire. I remember every ball of
it. Since then I've had to go by the papers. You seldom go to see cricket?

Charles Never.

Father Phipps Oh ... really? Well, gentlemen ...

He exits

Sebastian That was Father Phipps. He takes mass in our chapel. You're
C of E, aren't you?

Charles Oh, that's how I was brought up, certainly. But I have no
religion now.

Sebastian It's so very difficult being a Catholic ...

Charles Does it make much difference to you?

Sebastian Yes. All the time.

Charles Well, I can't say I've noticed it. You don't seem much more virtuous than me. I suppose they try and make you believe an awful lot of nonsense?

Sebastian Is it nonsense? I wish it were. It sometimes sounds very sensible to me.

Charles You can't seriously believe it all? About Christmas and the star for example, and the three kings, and the ox and the ass?

Sebastian Oh yes, I believe that. It's a lovely idea.

Charles You can't believe things because they're a lovely idea!

Sebastian But I do. That's how I believe!

Charles And you believe you can kneel down in front of a statue and say a few words, not even out loud, just in your mind, and change the weather; or that some saints are more influential than others, and you must get hold of the right one to help you on the right problem?

Sebastian Oh yes. Don't you remember last term I lost Aloysius? I prayed like mad to St Anthony of Padua that morning, and straight after lunch there was Mr Nichols, with Aloysius in his arms, saying I'd left him in his cab. (*He kisses and cuddles Aloysius*)

Charles Well, if you can believe that sort of thing, where's the difficulty in your religion?

Sebastian If you can't see, you can't.

Charles Well, where?

Sebastian Oh don't be a bore, Charles.

Charles You started the subject. I was just getting interested.

Sebastian I'll never mention it again ...

Sebastian wheels off

The Lights change to:

SCENE 11

The roof of Brideshead Castle. A bottle of wine and two glasses are set

We hear Sebastian laughing, off. Charles stands on one leg, also laughing

When Sebastian enters, hopping, we realize that Charles is imitating him

They jostle each other, then fall over

Charles I say! It's a wonderful view from here!
Sebastian Yes. I told you. Worth the climb, isn't it? We can sunbathe.
(*He begins to take his shirt off*) And when we get bored with the sun,
we can watch the quaint proceedings of the Agricultural show from
afar, like gods! You can see everything! Help yourself to wine.
Charles (*also taking his shirt off*) Is that why your brother is at
Brideshead? The show?
Sebastian Yes. Bridey's a big part of the Agricultural, so we're better off
hiding up here. (*He goes to look down*)
Charles Why?
Sebastian No-one will know where we are. No need to meet anyone.
Charles Your family, again?
Sebastian My brother. He's a queer fellow.

Charles joins him. Their naked torsos are very close

Charles He looks normal enough.
Sebastian Oh, but he's not. If you only knew, he's much the craziest of
us, only it doesn't come out at all. He's all twisted inside. He wanted
to be a priest. I think he still does. He nearly became a Jesuit. Poor
Mummy — the eldest son; it's not as if it had been me. And poor Papa.
The Church has been enough trouble to him without that.
Charles Has your father given up religion?
Sebastian Well, he's had to in a way; he only took to it when he married
Mummy. When he went off, he left that behind with the rest of us. So
you see, we're a mixed family religiously. Brideshead and Cordelia are
both fervent Catholics; he's miserable, she's bird-happy. Julia and I are
half-heathen. I'm happy, I rather think Julia isn't. Poor Mummy is
popularly believed to be a saint, and Papa is excommunicated — and
I wouldn't know which of *them* was happy! I wish I liked Catholics
more.
Charles They seem just like other people.
Sebastian (*putting his arm around Charles*) My dear Charles, that's
exactly what they're not. You see ——
Cordelia (*off*) Sebastian! Sebastian!
Sebastian Good heavens! That sounds like Cordelia. Cover yourself up.

Cordelia (*off*) Where are you?

Cordelia enters

Oh!

Sebastian Go away, Cordelia. We've got no clothes on.

Cordelia Why? You're quite decent. I guessed you were here. Darling Sebastian, I am pleased to see you again! How's your poor foot?

Sebastian Say "how d'you do" to Mr Ryder.

Cordelia Oh, sorry. How d'you do. I thought I'd better tell you Bridey's coming up.

Sebastian What?

Cordelia He asked me where you were, and I made a guess. I've run ahead to warn you. I say, who's been painting the office?

Sebastian Be careful what you say. It's Mr Ryder.

Cordelia But it's lovely. I say, did you really? You are clever.

Brideshead enters

Brideshead Ah, there you are ... Quite a view from here, don't you think, Mr Ryder?

Charles Yes ... we were looking at the show.

Brideshead Thank goodness my duty's done for the day! So many hands to shake. I hope Sebastian is looking after you properly? You are fond of wine?

Charles Very.

Brideshead I wish I were. It's such a bond with other men.

Cordelia I like wine.

Brideshead Cordelia's report said that she was not only the worst girl in the school, but the worst there had ever been in the memory of the oldest nun.

Cordelia That's because I refused to be an Enfant de Marie! Reverend Mother said that if I didn't keep my room tidier I couldn't be one. I said that I didn't believe Our Blessed Lady cared two hoots whether I put my gym shoes on the left or right of my dancing shoes. Reverend Mother was livid.

Brideshead Our Lady cares about obedience.

Sebastian Bridey, you mustn't be pious. We've got an atheist with us.

Charles Agnostic.

Brideshead I saw the Bishop in London last week. You know, he wants to close our chapel and open a mass centre at Melstead.

Cordelia Oh, but we'd have to travel — and I like popping in at odd times. So does Mummy.

Brideshead So do I. But there are so few of us.

Cordelia I think it's beautiful.

Brideshead (*to Charles*) Is it good art, the chapel?

Charles Well, I don't know what you mean. Probably in eighty years it will be greatly admired.

Brideshead But surely it can't be good in eighty years time and not good now?

Charles Well it may be good now. All I mean is I don't happen to like it much.

Brideshead But is there a difference between liking a thing and thinking it good?

Sebastian Bridey, don't be so Jesuitical.

Brideshead I'm sorry. I thought it rather an interesting point. However, I need to take Sebastian aside for a minute. I've some papers for Father to sign. Sebastian must take them to Venice and explain them to him.

Cordelia It's all right. I'll talk to Charles.

Sebastian Charles? *Charles*? "Mr Ryder" to you, child.

He goes to one side with Brideshead

Cordelia Come on, Charles.

She leads him by the hand, and they sit apart from the other two

Are you really agnostic?

Charles Does your family talk about religion all the time?

Cordelia Not all the time. It's a subject that just comes up naturally, doesn't it?

Charles Does it? It never has with me before.

Cordelia Then perhaps you are an agnostic. I'll pray for you.

Charles That's very kind of you.

Cordelia I can't spare a whole rosary, you know. Just a decade. I've got such a long list of people. I take them in order and they get a decade about once a week.

Charles I'm sure it's more than I deserve.

Cordelia Oh, I've got some harder cases than you. There's the Kaiser,
Lloyd George, Olive Banks ——
Charles Who's she?
Cordelia She was bunked from the convent last term. I don't quite know
what for. Reverend Mother found something she'd been writing.
D'you know, if you weren't agnostic, I should ask you for five shillings
to buy a black god-daughter. You send five bob to some nuns in Africa
and they christen a baby and name her after you. I've got six black
Cordelias already. Isn't it lovely?

Brideshead and Sebastian walk back

Brideshead Have you two been getting along?
Charles Cordelia has promised to pray for me.
Sebastian I wouldn't be too flattered — she prayed for nine days for her
pig!
Brideshead I think we're causing scandal. Come along, Cordelia.
Cordelia Once a week, I promise.

Brideshead and Cordelia exit

Charles You know, all this is very puzzling for me.
Sebastian Of course. I did warn you. I think you'd better come with me
to Venice. Meet Papa and Cara.
Charles I've no money.
Sebastian I thought of that. We live on Papa when we get there, and the
lawyers pay enough for my first-class fare and sleeper — we can both
travel third for that. We can take the cheap sea-crossing to Dunkirk,
make for Paris in one of those wooden-seated trains, and then change
at Milan.
Charles It'll be uncomfortable.
Sebastian It'll be fun! We can sit all night on the deck of the ferry and
watch England disappear, and France welcome us! We'll have a stroll
around Paris, make for the Gare de Lyon, and then head south. Oh,
Charles! The heat, the olives, the vines ... and then, last and best of all,
the city of light — Venice! Will you come?
Charles (*laughing*) Why not?

They link arms, pick up a small bag each, and walk

The Lights cross-fade to:

SCENE 12

Music. We are in Venice

Sebastian I gather Papa's alone at the moment. No need to dress for dinner.

They walk in

Lord Marchmain enters

Lord Marchmain Sebastian, Sebastian.

They embrace. Sebastian kisses his father on the cheek

Sebastian Darling Papa! How young you're looking! This is Charles. Don't you think my father very handsome, Charles?

Lord Marchmain and Charles shake hands

Lord Marchmain Whoever looked up your train made a *bêtise*. There is no such one.
Sebastian (*with a wink at Charles*) We came on it.
Lord Marchmain There was only a slow train from Milan at that time. I hope you boys will be fairly comfortable upstairs. I have a room, and Cara has the other sizeable one ... but no doubt we shall manage.
Sebastian How is Cara?
Lord Marchmain Well, I hope. I expect her back at any moment. She's been visiting some American friends at a villa on the Brenta canal. Now, how do you plan your time here? Bathing or sightseeing?
Charles Some sightseeing, anyway, I hope.
Lord Marchmain Cara will like that. I would stick to the churches. Avoid the Lido.
Sebastian Charles is very keen on painting.
Lord Marchmain Yes? Any particular Venetian painter?
Charles Bellini.
Lord Marchmain Yes? Which?
Charles I'm afraid I didn't know there were two of them.
Lord Marchmain Three, to be precise. The Italian painters liked to keep it in the family. How did you leave England?

Sebastian It's been lovely.

Lord Marchmain Has it? It's been my tragedy that I abominate the English countryside. I suppose it is a disgraceful thing to inherit great responsibilities and to be entirely indifferent to them. I am all the Socialists would have me to be, and a great stumbling-block to my own party. Well, my elder son will change all that, I've no doubt, if they leave him anything to inherit.

Cara enters

Ah, Cara my dear. We have visitors from England!

Cara Sebastian! How lovely to see you again.

They embrace and kiss

Sebastian This is my friend, Charles.

Cara Mr Ryder, isn't it? We have been told. Delighted to meet you. An artist, we understand?

Charles Well — hardly ... yet.

Cara There are lots of beautiful things to see here. Oh, Vittoria Corombona has asked us all to her ball on Saturday.

Lord Marchmain It's very kind of her, but you know I do not dance.

Cara But for the boys? It is a thing to be seen — the Corombona Palace all lit up...

Lord Marchmain The boys can do as they like. We must refuse.

Cara There is a charming daughter ... Sebastian and his friend will like her.

Lord Marchmain Sebastian and his friend are more interested in Bellini than heiresses. They want to see the treasures of Venice.

He exits, beckoning to Sebastian

Sebastian picks up both bags and starts to exit, then stops at the doorway to look back at Charles

Cara Oh! But that is what I have always wished! I have not been to San Marco, even. Alex never explores! We will become tourists, yes?

Charles (*with a look at Sebastian*) Yes! Yes, please.

Sebastian smiles and exits

Cara I think you are very fond of Sebastian?

Charles Why, certainly.

Cara I know of these romantic friendships of the English and the Germans. They are not Latin. I think they are very good if they do not go on too long. It is a kind of love that comes to children before they know its meaning. It is better to have that kind of love for another boy than for a girl. Alex, you see, had it for a girl; for his wife. But now he hates her. You can have no conception how he hates her. He will not set foot in England because it is her home. But Sebastian ... he is in love with his own childhood — his teddy bear, his Nanny. And he drinks too much.

Charles I suppose we both do.

Cara With you it does not matter. With Sebastian it is different. He will be a drunkard if someone does not come and stop him. It's in the blood ... Someone must stop him, or it will be too late ... too late ... too late ...

She walks away and exits, as if fading from Charles's memory

He turns and sits on a chair. He is back at Oxford. The Lights change to:

SCENE 13

Charles's rooms at Oxford

Music. A wind blows; Oxford bells toll

Sebastian enters with Aloysius and a bottle. He sits Aloysius down in a chair

Charles is reading

Sebastian I feel precisely one hundred years old! Typical of Oxford to start the new year in autumn.

Charles Good-morning, Sebastian.

Sebastian Yes, but it isn't! I've just had a talking-to from Monseigneur Bell. That makes the fourth since I came up. First my tutor, then the Rural Dean, then the obnoxious Mr Samgrass of All Souls ——

Charles Who or what is Mr Samgrass of All Souls?

Sebastian Someone of Mummy's.

Charles Oh, yes. I remember. It's the don that she's come up to see.

Sebastian She's getting him to edit a memorial book about her brother Ned — killed at Passchendaele, you know. There's some papers, poems, letters, speeches.

Charles Why choose Samgrass?

Sebastian Apparently it's something he does.

Charles And your mother has asked him to lecture you as part of the deal?

Sebastian So it seems. She can be very persuasive.

Charles She is charming.

Sebastian Oh, we all are, curse us! She's taken to you, I'm afraid. Be warned. She means business.

Charles I don't know what you mean.

Julia enters

Julia Ah, I've found you, Sebastian!

Sebastian Julia! This is a surprise! What are you doing here?

Julia Sorry I didn't let you know I was coming, but I brought Mr Mottram with me. Come in, Rex ...

Rex Mottram enters

You know Sebastian, of course. This is his friend, Mr Ryder — Charles.

Charles How do you do.

Rex Well, thank you. Very well!

Julia Except that we've been starved for a week.

Sebastian Starved?

Julia We've been staying at the Chasms. Simply awful. We hoped Sebastian might give us lunch and we guessed he was here. If it's inconvenient we'll try Boy Mulcaster.

Charles Oh! He and Sebastian are both lunching with me. Come too. We've a table booked at the Trout.

Rex Oh, yes. An interesting little place. Know it well.

Charles Were you here? At Oxford?

Rex Oh, no. I'm not a university man. And I think it shows. It means you start life three years behind the other fellow. My formative years were spent at the racetrack and on the golf course. That's how I got to meet the people who really count in this world! No, the secluded grove of academe is not for me.

Charles So, what sort of life do you lead?

Julia Rex is a Member of Parliament, so he spends most of his time in London.

Charles Ah, I see...

Rex London is the hub — it's full of the people who have made it, who mean something. That's where to be, that's where contacts are to be made. I've got a charity ball up there in a week's time. Consider yourself invited. Lots of important people ...

Charles Thank you. I'm sure we'll think about it.

Rex Oh, but there's nothing to think about. Come to dinner with me first.
And bring that Mulcaster fellow too. Well, now ... are we going to eat
or not? I'll go and fetch the car round and we can drive over.

He exits

Julia I'm sorry. He's not quite as embarrassing as he seems. Remember,
he's a colonial. I'd better go and guide him round.

She exits

Sebastian What do you think?

Charles About Rex Mottram?

Sebastian This charity ball. Shall we go? I don't think he knows anyone
young. All his friends are leathery old sharks in the City and the House
of Commons.

Charles Why does he want Boy Mulcaster?

Sebastian Julia and I have known Boy all our lives. I suppose, hearing
he was lunching with us, Mottram thought that he was a chum. Let's go
anyway. It might be fun ...

*Music begins. A dance/movement sequence follows, in which Sebastian,
Charles and Boy Mulcaster have drinks and dance with each other. They then
dance with Rex (much to his annoyance) and finally spin off, taking Rex's
bottle with them. This forms the link into:*

SCENE 14

London

Boy Mulcaster enters, drunk

Mulcaster Come on! This way ...

Sebastian Where are we going?

Mulcaster I told you I'd show you somewhere better than that dull old
ball — we're going to Ma Mayfield's!

Charles Who is Ma Mayfield?

Mulcaster Ma Mayfield at the Old Hundredth. I've got a regular, here.
Sweet little thing called Effie. (*He walks up to the door*)

Ma Mayfield opens the door and comes out

Ma Mayfield Members?
Mulcaster I like that! You ought to know me by now.
Ma Mayfield Yes, dearie. Ten bob each.
Mulcaster Oh, now look here, I've never paid before.
Ma Mayfield Daresay not, dearie. We're full up tonight, so it's ten bob.
Anyone comes after you will have to pay a quid. You're lucky.
Mulcaster Let me speak to Mrs Mayfield.
Ma Mayfield I *am* Mrs Mayfield. Ten bob each.
Mulcaster Why, Ma, I didn't recognize you in all your finery. You know
me, don't you? Boy Mulcaster.
Ma Mayfield Yes, duckie. Ten bob each.

They pay their money over

Ta, dear.
Mulcaster Where's Effie tonight?
Ma Mayfield Effie 'oo?
Mulcaster Effie. One of the girls who's always here. The pretty dark one.
Ma Mayfield There's lots of girls works here. Some of them's dark,
some of them's fair. I haven't the time to know them by name.

She exits into the house. Effie enters and walks past

Mulcaster There she is! Effie! Effie!
Effie Me?
Mulcaster It's me, Boy!
Effie Oh ...
Mulcaster Come and meet my chums — Charles and Sebastian ...
Effie Charmed, I'm sure. (*To Charles*) I've seen you here before, haven't
I?
Charles I'm afraid not.
Effie (*to Sebastian*) What about you? Have I had the pleasure ...?
Sebastian I rather think not.
Effie Oh. (*To Mulcaster*) But I've seen you before ... haven't I?
Mulcaster Well, I should rather hope so. You haven't forgotten our little
evening in September?
Effie No, darling. You were the boy in the Guards who cut your toe
weren't you?
Mulcaster Now, Effie — don't be a tease.
Effie I know. You were with Bunty the time the police were in and we
all hid behind the dustbins ...
Mulcaster Effie loves pulling my leg.

Effie Whatever you say, I know I have seen you before somewhere. D'you wanna dance?

Mulcaster Not at the minute.

Effie Thank the Lord. My shoes pinch something terrible tonight.

Mulcaster Tell you what. Let's all go for a drive!

Effie What, with the three of yer?

Mulcaster Of course!

Effie Tell you what. I've got a couple of friends live just down the way. They'd like to meet your mates.

Mulcaster Splendid! We'll all have a good time.

Effie Yeah. But listen — you can't drive in that state.

Mulcaster 'S all right. Sebastian's a good driver. And he can take his drink, you see. Come on, Sebastian. Drive us into the welcoming night ...

Effie puts her arm around Mulcaster and they all begin to move off

A Policeman enters and stops Sebastian

Policeman Just a minute, sir. What are you doing?

Sebastian We are going about our legitimate business, what does it look like?

Policeman Is that your vehicle over there?

Sebastian No. It's his. (*He points to Mulcaster*)

Policeman I see. And were any of you preparing to drive it, sir? Because if you were, I would have to advise you against it.

Sebastian Your advice, officer has been duly noted. But, after weighty consideration, it will be ignored.

Policeman Now, come on, sir. We don't want a charge of drunk and disorderly, do we sir?

Sebastian I can only speak for myself, I'm afraid. I wouldn't attempt to guess what you want. Now please let me pass. As you see, I have my passengers to consider.

Policeman Now just hold on. (*He looks at Effie*) 'Ere, I know you ...

Effie lets go of Mulcaster and runs off

Mulcaster Now look what you've done! You've frightened Effie! Come on, Sebastian, let's get in the car and go after her.

Sebastian exits

Policeman I think not, sir.

Mulcaster Go on, Sebastian! You get in. I'll hold the bobby!

He struggles with the Policeman. Charles is in the mêlée in a drunken stupor. We hear a car start and crash. They all freeze, and the Policeman wrenches himself free as they stare off

Policeman Right, gentlemen. I didn't want to take all this trouble, but now I'll have to ask you to accompany me to the station.

Sebastian staggers on

Sebastian I'm not drunk. The clutch slipped. I tell you I'm not drunk. Oh, Charles ... I suppose Mummy's got to hear about all this?
Policeman Come on, sir.

Music

The Policeman leads Sebastian off, followed by Mulcaster and Charles

The Lights cross-fade to:

SCENE 15

The Brideshead setting

Lady Marchmain sits working at an embroidery hoop

Julia Mummy! I can't get into the library.
Lady Marchmain No? Well, I expect Mr Samgrass is in there, researching.
Julia Why does he have to lock the door?
Lady Marchmain I expect he doesn't want to be disturbed, dear.
Julia Yes, but it's our library. It's uncomfortable having a part of our home taken over. It's not the first time.
Lady Marchmain After what he did for Sebastian in the magistrate's court, we should all be very grateful to Mr Samgrass. His evidence of good character was so helpful.
Julia I can't help thinking he overdid it a bit. And he didn't stop Sebastian and Boy and Charles being gated, did he?
Lady Marchmain No. There was no reason why he should. And anyway, it kept them out of mischief for a while. I only hope Sebastian has learned from the experience. There! Nearly done. It's for the chapel. What do you think? I just need to fetch some green thread, so

if you really want to go into the library, I'll ask Mr Samgrass to open the door ——

Samgrass enters

Oh! There you are. Have you had a successful morning, Mr Samgrass?
Samgrass Fascinating, fascinating. My research is almost complete. I hope to start writing next week.
Lady Marchmain How exciting. Er — it won't disturb your papers and things if Julia goes into the library now, will it?
Samgrass Oh no ... no. Everything's tidy.
Lady Marchmain Good. Come along then, Julia.

Julia and Lady Marchmain exit

Samgrass starts to go out opposite

Charles enters

Samgrass Ah, Ryder. Lady Marchmain told me you'd arrived this morning. I've been hidden away, you see — researching in the library. It's all arrivals and departures! Lady Julia is leaving tomorrow with her friend Celia to celebrate the New Year elsewhere. But I shall stay and continue my work on our hostess's book. Ah well, the hour of cocktails is very nearly upon us. I shall be ready to answer the summons.

He exits. Lady Marchmain enters

Lady Marchmain Charles! How are you? I haven't had the chance to speak to you since you got here. It is good of you to share some of your holiday with us. You left your father well I trust?
Charles Thank you, yes. I didn't see him much. It is generous of you to allow me to stay again.
Lady Marchmain Generous? What nonsense. Sebastian wouldn't be without you, you know, and I'm sure the rest of us simply regard you as one of the family. Besides which, we seem to benefit each time you stay by acquiring yet another painting in the garden room.
Charles Oh, they're just a bit of fun. They hardly compare with the lovely things elsewhere in your house. You have so much here.
Lady Marchmain Yes. You know, I used to think it wrong to have so many beautiful things when others had nothing.
Charles Wrong?

Lady Marchmain I used to think so. But I believe it is one of the special achievements of Grace to sanctify the whole of life — after all, the poor have always been the favourites of God and his saints. There is a balance, you see.

Charles It doesn't concern you that we are told that it's easier for a camel to pass through the eye of a needle than for a rich man to enter the kingdom of God?

Lady Marchmain Not at all. The gospel is simply a *catalogue* of unexpected things! It's not to be expected that an ox and an ass should worship at the crib. Animals are always doing the oddest things in the lives of the saints. It's all part of the poetry, the Alice-in-Wonderland side of religion. Don't look so dumbfounded. (*She picks up her embroidery hoop*) We must make a Catholic of you, Charles. We really must. Then you'll understand.

She exits. Sebastian enters, drunk. He holds a bottle of whisky behind his back

Sebastian Has Mummy been having one of her "little talks" with you? She's always doing it. I wish she wouldn't.

Charles It's all right. I took her on.

Sebastian Haven't they brought the cocktails yet?

Charles No. Where have you been all day? I was looking for you.

Sebastian I ... got sick of being grateful to old Samgrass. I've been up with Nanny.

Charles I don't believe it. You've been drinking somewhere.

Sebastian I've been reading in my room. My cold's terrible today. I needed a drink to drive it away. I think I'd better have something-on-a-tray upstairs. Not dinner with Mummy.

Charles Go to bed. I'll say your cold's worse.

Sebastian Much worse. (*He shows Charles the whisky bottle he's been holding behind him*)

Charles (*trying unsuccessfully to take the bottle from him*) Don't be an ass, Sebastian. You've had enough.

Sebastian What the devil's it got to do with you? You're only a guest here — my guest! I drink what I want to in my own house!!

Charles Well, for God's sake keep out of sight!

Sebastian Oh, mind your own business! You came here as my friend; now you're spying on me for my mother, I know!

Charles No, Sebastian ——

Sebastian Well you can get out! And tell her from me that I'll choose my friends and she her spies in future!

He exits

Lady Marchmain, Julia and Brideshead enter

Lady Marchmain (*looking around*) Oh, I thought I heard Sebastian. Is anything wrong?
Charles He has a cold — he's gone to bed. He says he doesn't want anything.
Lady Marchmain Poor Sebastian. He'd better have glass of hot whisky. I'll go and have a look at him.
Julia It's all right, Mummy! I'll go —— (*She starts to go*)

Cordelia enters

Cordelia Where are you going? To see our invalid?
Julia Mummy's concerned about Sebastian.
Cordelia Oh! I shouldn't worry. I've just passed him on the stairs. I shouldn't think he wants anything.
Lady Marchmain How was he?
Cordelia Well, I don't know, but I think he's very drunk. (*She laughs*) "Marquis' Son Unused to Wine", "Model Student's Career Threatened."
Lady Marchmain Charles, is this true?
Charles Yes.
Lady Marchmain I see. We must change for dinner.

The ladies exit

Brideshead stops Charles

Brideshead Drunk?
Charles I'm afraid so, yes.
Brideshead Extraordinary time to choose. Couldn't you stop him?
Charles No.
Brideshead (*looking at him*) No. I don't suppose you could. I once saw my father drunk, in this very room. I wasn't more than about ten at the time. I shall ask mother to read to us tonight, after dinner. We always ask her to read aloud when things ... aren't quite right. From *The Wisdom of Father Brown*, usually. It's a family favourite. (*He starts to exit, then turns to Charles*) My mother couldn't stop my father, you know. You can't stop people if they want to get drunk.

He exits

Sebastian puts his head around the door and looks around the room

Sebastian Come to apologize. I was bloody to you, and you're my guest.
You're my guest and my only friend, and I was bloody to you.
Charles You'd better get back to your room.
Sebastian Why do you take their side against me? Why do you do that?
Charles I don't. I really don't! When we get back to Oxford, I'll help you
all I can. You must know that.
Sebastian (*bitterly*) Must I?
Charles Sebastian! I'm with you, *contra mundum.*
Sebastian (*looking unsteadily at Charles*) Yes. Yes, of course you are.
(*With great sadness*) Good-night.

He exits

The Lights fade until it is very dark, and we hear clock chimes

*Sebastian staggers on totally drunk, holding a bottle. He stops, wobbles a
bit, then begins to sing with the chimes: "Samgrass, green arse, green arse,
Samgrass"*

A Tutor enters and takes the bottle from Sebastian

*Sebastian staggers to a halt, and finally flops into a chair. The Lights come
up on:*

SCENE 16

Sebastian's Oxford study. Daytime

Charles Sebastian, why? I mean, what an extraordinarily foolish thing
to do!
Sebastian I know.
Charles I mean, getting drunk just because your mother came to see you
— that's silly enough. But getting caught at one in the morning by the
Junior Dean in the quad unable to control yourself ... you'll be sent
down. It's inevitable.
Sebastian You see it's only when they start bothering me. It'd be all right
if they'd only leave me alone.
Charles They won't now.
Sebastian I know.
Charles Really, if you are going to embark on a solitary bout of drinking
every time you see a member of your family, it's hopeless.

Sebastian Oh, yes. I know. It's hopeless.

Charles I told your mother I really thought you'd stopped. It makes me look a liar.

Sebastian "*Contra mundum*", Charles?

Charles I meant I would stand with you. Help you fight it.

Sebastian Oh, for God's sake, Charles! I can get that kind of help from my family. I said I'd go and live with Papa in Venice if they sent me down, but Mummy says she wants Samgrass — Samgrass, Charles! — to take me to the Levant and just ... tour about!

Charles God, what a prospect! (*He goes to him*)

Sebastian (*looking at Charles with enormous sadness*) I knew what would happen to us if Mummy started her "little talks" with you.

Charles Sebastian, what do you mean? Nothing's happened! All right, you'll be sent down, and you'll have to pay the penalty and put up with Samgrass breathing down your neck for a while, but that doesn't affect us. Nothing's happened between us!

Sebastian (*looking at him*) Is that what you think?

Charles Yes! (*Unsure now*) Don't you? (*Looking for the response that won't come*) *Contra mundum*, Sebastian!

Soft music begins

Sebastian Oh, Charles! We had so little time! (*He embraces Charles*) Bless you, Charles! Bless you! (*He is crying*)

They hold each other tightly. As the Lights fade, Sebastian drops Aloysius to the floor

SCENE 17

Mr Ryder's house

The music fades. When the Lights come up we see Charles deep in thought

Charles's father enters

Mr Ryder Ah, there you are. Home again. Er ... that very good-looking friend of yours. Is he not with you?

Charles No. He's ... he had a very bad term. Both of us, actually.

Mr Ryder I'm sorry to hear that. You didn't tell me you'd been in trouble.

Charles Not in trouble, Father. Not directly. It was Sebastian.

Mr Ryder Yes?

Charles I'm afraid he's been sent down.

Mr Ryder Ah ...

Charles He's in the Levant.

Mr Ryder Didn't you consider going with him?

Charles No. I ... I couldn't. (*Pause*) He may not come again.

Mr Ryder I'm sorry. I liked him.

Charles Father, do you particularly want me to take my degree?

Mr Ryder *I* want you to? No use to me. Not much use to you, either, as far as I've seen.

Charles That's exactly what I've been thinking. I think it will be best if I start now on what I intend doing. I want to be a painter.

Mr Ryder A painter? Really? But you'll need a studio.

Charles Yes.

Mr Ryder Well, there isn't a studio here, or even a room you could decently use as a studio. And I won't have undraped models all over the house, nor critics with their horrible jargon ...

Charles I was thinking of working at an art school, if you agree to my leaving Oxford.

Mr Ryder Agree? Agree? My dear boy, you're twenty-two!

Charles Twenty. Twenty-one in October.

Mr Ryder Is that all? It seems much longer.

Charles Yes. Yes it does.

Mr Ryder There are some excellent schools abroad, I believe. Is that what you'll do? Go abroad?

Charles Abroad or here. I'll have to look round first.

Mr Ryder Yes, of course. I should look round abroad.

He exits

Charles Yes ... yes, I will ... (*He closes his eyes*) Oh! Sebastian! Sebastian!

He begins to cry as the music begins and swells. He turns to look at Aloysius lying on the floor

The Lights fade, with a final spot on Aloysius; then that, too, goes out

CURTAIN

ACT II
SCENE 1

Brideshead

Music. When the Lights come up, we see Charles standing dressed in his army greatcoat and holding his clipboard, as before. The Flyte family is once more revealed behind the gauze, in photographic pose; Sebastian holds a bottle

The Lights change again, and the members of the group melt into their positions for looking at the Levant trip photographs. As this is set up, Charles removes his greatcoat, walks into the scene, and sits

Samgrass And when we reached the top of the pass, we heard the sound of galloping horses behind us, and two soldiers rode up. You know they turned us back just in time — there was a band, not a mile ahead!

Julia A band? Goodness!

Lady Marchmain I suppose the sort of folk music you get in those parts is rather monotonous.

Samgrass Dear Lady Marchmain, a band of brigands! The mountains are full of them. Very desperate fellows, I assure you!

Julia So you never got to wherever-it-was? Weren't you terribly disappointed, Sebastian?

Sebastian Me? Oh ... I don't think I was there that day, was I, Sammy?

Samgrass That was the day you were ill.

Sebastian I was ill, so I never should have got to wherever-it-was, should I, Sammy?

Samgrass Now this (*he passes the photograph to Lady Marchmain*) is the caravan at Aleppo in the courtyard of the inn, and the others are of fellow travellers at various places ——

Cordelia All guides and mules and ruins. Where's Sebastian?

Samgrass Ah! He held the camera. He became quite an expert when he learned not to put his hand over the lens, didn't you, Sebastian? Now this is a group taken by a street photographer ——

Charles Why, there's Anthony Blanche, surely?

Samgrass Met him by chance at Constantinople. A delightful companion. He came with us all the way to Beirut.

Lady Marchmain Well, now. It's been most interesting seeing what fun you and Sebastian had together. I think I shall take tea in my room in a while. Would you like to join me, Mr Samgrass?

Samgrass Oh ... yes, of course.

Lady Marchmain Just a little talk ... There are one or two things I want to ask you about.

Samgrass Why yes. Delighted, delighted. I'll just get these photographs put away.

Lady Marchmain and Samgrass exit in different directions

Cordelia Aren't you pleased to be home, Sebastian?

Sebastian Of course I'm pleased.

Cordelia Well you might show it. I've been looking forward to it so much. Nanny Hawkins is right. You are looking peaky. Not well at all.

Sebastian I'm all right. How is Paris, Charles? And the art school?

Charles The teachers are good — the old ones, anyway. But I can't say the same for the students. They all want to do advertisements for *Vogue*, and the teachers try to make them paint like Delacroix!

Cordelia Charles. Modern art is all bosh, isn't it?

Charles Great bosh.

Cordelia Oh! I'm so glad! I had an argument with one of our nuns, and she said we shouldn't criticize what we didn't understand. Now I shall tell her that I have had it straight from a real artist, and snubs to her!

She exits

Sebastian I say! Where's the cocktail things? They're usually about by now. Can't understand it. Oh, well, I'll go and see what I can find ...

He exits

Brideshead Charles. There's something we've got to explain. My mother has given orders that no drinks are to be left in any of the rooms. You'll understand why. If you want anything, ring and ask Wilcox — only better wait until you're alone. I'm sorry, but there it is.

Charles Is that necessary?

Brideshead I gather very necessary. You may or may not have heard: Sebastian had another outbreak as soon as he got back to England. He was lost over Christmas. Mr Samgrass only found him yesterday evening. He had to tell Mummy.

Charles I guessed something like that had happened, but are you sure this is the best way of dealing with it?

Brideshead It's my mother's way. Will you have a cocktail now that he's gone upstairs?
Charles It would choke me.
Brideshead It's for his own good.

Brideshead exits

Julia So now we've all got to keep an eye on him. It's too tedious. Why can't he behave like anyone else?
Charles You could make things worse ...
Julia They're awful now. The servants have been instructed not to give him a drink unless Mummy sanctions it — even at dinner. And talking of keeping an eye on people, what about Mr Samgrass? Charles, do you notice anything at all fishy about that man?
Charles Very fishy. Do you think your mother saw it?
Julia Mummy only sees what suits her. She can't have the whole household under surveillance. I'm causing anxiety, too, you know.
Charles I didn't know. I've only just come from Paris.

Lady Marchmain enters with Brideshead

Lady Marchmain Bridey's just reminded me that there's a hunt tomorrow. Are you riding out, Julia?
Julia No. I told you, Mummy. I'm expecting Rex.
Lady Marchmain Oh. What about Cordelia?
Brideshead Yes, she's coming. And I'm taking Julia's young horse to show him the hounds.

Sebastian enters and stands at the door

Sebastian Where's the meet?
Julia Just here at Flyte St Mary.
Sebastian Then I'd like to hunt, please, if there's anything for me.
Brideshead Of course. That's delightful! I'd have asked you, only you always used to complain so of being made to go out. You can have Tinkerbell. She's been going very nicely this season. I'm going to get the whisky. Anyone else want any?
Sebastian Yes, please.

Brideshead looks at Lady Marchmain. She nods

Brideshead exits

Lady Marchmain Come along Julia. I want to have a word with you, and then I really must see Mr Samgrass. Have you any idea where he's got to? You don't think he can be avoiding me, do you?

She offers her arm, they exit

Charles I rather wish I was coming out with you tomorrow.

Sebastian Well, you wouldn't see much sport. I can tell you exactly what I'm going to do. I shall leave Bridey at the first covert, hack over to the nearest good pub, and spend the morning quietly soaking in the bar parlour. If they treat me like a dipsomaniac, they can bloody well have a dipsomaniac. I hate hunting, anyway.

Charles Well, I can't stop you.

Sebastian You can, as a matter of fact. By not giving me any money. They stopped my banking account, you know, in the summer. I pawned my watch and cigarette case to ensure a happy Christmas. I shall have to come to you for tomorrow's expenses.

Charles I can't ... you know I can't ...

Sebastian Can't you? Well, I'll just manage on my own, then. I've got rather clever at that, lately. I've had to.

Charles Sebastian. What have you and Samgrass been up to?

Sebastian Ruins and guides and mules — that's what Samgrass has been up to. We decided to go our own ways, that's all. You see, I got lucky and made some cash at cards in Constantinople, when Sammy wasn't looking. Then I made my own way South. I cabled Samgrass to let him know I was quite well and could he send money regularly. And bless him, so he did. Sammy really behaved rather well. I hoped he would keep it up, but he seems to have been very indiscreet about my happy Christmas. I suppose he thought if he gave too good an account of me he might lose his job as keeper. He does rather well out of it. Anyway, I met up with him by appointment in Syria three weeks ago and we came back to England.

Charles But not to Brideshead.

Sebastian I was determined to have a happy Christmas.

Charles Did you?

Sebastian I think so. I don't remember it much, and that's always a good sign, isn't it? Then back to this. Charles, you've seen the way they want to treat me. You won't refuse me just a little money? I must escape ... I must.

Charles Oh ... Sebastian ... (*He opens his wallet and gives him a note*)

Sebastian A pound? Charles ... please.

Charles passes his wallet to Sebastian with an air of resignation. Sebastian takes a five pound note from it. They look at each other

The Lights cross-fade to:

SCENE 2

Music

We see the family out hunting, represented by a dance sequence. Sebastian rides off away from the others after a while

The Lights change again at the end of the music, and we are back at Brideshead

Lady Marchmain I've always detested hunting, because it seems to produce a particularly gross kind of caddishness in the nicest people ... and yet, you know — it must be something derived from centuries ago — my heart is quite light today to think of Sebastian out with them. "There's nothing wrong with him, really", I say, "he's gone hunting" — as though it were an answer to prayer. What are your plans when you leave here, Charles? Paris again, I suppose?

Charles I shall spend a few days in London before I go back. I hope Sebastian will come to stay with me. My father would like it.

Lady Marchmain Charles, you know that isn't possible. London's the worst place. Even Mr Samgrass couldn't hold him there. He was lost, you know, and Mr Samgrass only found him because he couldn't pay his bill, so they telephoned our house. No, we must keep him happy and healthy here, for a bit, hunting, and then send him abroad again with Mr Samgrass ... you see, I've been through all this before ... I hope he's having a good day ...

Brideshead enters

Ah, the first back. Had a good morning?

Brideshead Yes, thanks. Good sport.

Lady Marchmain Are the others coming?

Brideshead Oh, Cordelia wasn't far away. Haven't seen anything of Sebastian since first thing.

Lady Marchmain goes off to look out of a window. Brideshead leads Charles aside

Charles ... Sebastian — is it dipsomania, do you think? I hope so. That is simply a great misfortune that we must all help him to bear. What I used to fear was that he just got drunk deliberately when he liked and because he liked.

Charles That's exactly what he did — what we both did. It's what he does
with me now. I can keep him to that, if only your mother would trust me.
If you worry him with keepers and cures he'll be a physical wreck in a few
years.

Brideshead There's nothing wrong in being a physical wreck, you know.
There's no moral obligation to live to walk ten miles at eighty.

Charles "Wrong"? "Moral obligation"? You're back on religion again.

Brideshead I never left it.

Julia bursts in, carrying a box — she is followed by Rex Mottram

Julia Mummy! Do look at Rex's Christmas present.

Lady Marchmain (*looking in the box*) A tortoise? But what's that stuck in
its shell?

Julia My initials — see, "J.F.", you see? In diamonds!

Lady Marchmain How ... unusual. I wonder ... does it eat the same sort of
things as an ordinary tortoise?

Rex It was just a bit of fun.

Julia It's lovely.

Lady Marchmain Have you warned Mr Mottram about ... our little
problem, Julia?

Julia Sebastian? Oh, yes. Actually, Rex had an idea about that, didn't you
Rex?

Rex Yes. Bovethus is the man. Sanatorium at Zurich. Works miracles. You
know how Charlie Kilcartney used to drink.

Lady Marchmain No, I'm afraid I don't.

Rex Two wives despaired of him. When he got engaged to Sylvia, she made
it a condition that he should take the cure at Zurich. And it worked. He came
back in three months a different man. And he hasn't touched a drop since,
even though Sylvia walked out on him.

Lady Marchmain Why did she do that?

Rex Well, poor Charlie got rather a bore when he stopped drinking. But
that's not really the point of the story.

Lady Marchmain No, I suppose not. In fact, I suppose, it's meant to be an
encouraging story.

Rex He takes sex cases, too, you know.

Lady Marchmain Oh dear, what very peculiar friends poor Sebastian will
make in Zurich.

Rex He's booked up for months ahead, but I think he'd find room if I asked
him.

Cordelia enters

Lady Marchmain Well, it certainly seems that we should consider it.
Cordelia Consider what, Mummy? Oh, Julia! What's that in there? How
    beastly!
Julia It's Rex's Christmas present.
Cordelia Oh, sorry, I'm always putting my foot in it. But how cruel! It must
    have hurt frightfully.
Julia They can't feel.
Cordelia How do you know? I bet they can. Oh — I've just been looking
    at Bobbin, I think he may have jarred his leg, but what a spiffing day! Jean
    Strickland-Venables fell in the mud. Terrific! And we ran from Bengers to
    Upper Rastney without a check. I reckon that's five miles, don't you,
    Bridey?
Lady Marchmain Where's Sebastian?
Cordelia Isn't he back? I expect he got lost.

Sebastian laughs off stage. The family turn to him

He enters, obviously only just holding himself steady

There is an awkward silence for a second or two

Lady Marchmain Dear boy! There you are! How nice to see you looking
    so well again. Your morning in the open has done you good. The drinks are
    on the table through there. Do help yourself.
Sebastian Thanks, I will. (*He goes to the drinks*)
Charles (*following him*) Sebastian, tell me. Tell me honestly ...
Sebastian What? Tell you what?
Charles Do you want me to stay on here?
Sebastian Stay?
Charles I'm no help, am I? No help at all.
Sebastian No. You're no help. (*Deliberately loudly*) There's your change.
    Thanks.

He takes his drink and exits

*Charles moves back, to be stopped by Lady Marchmain. She is very
distressed*

Lady Marchmain Charles. There's something I must ask you. Did you give
    Sebastian money?
Charles Yes.
Lady Marchmain Knowing how he was likely to spend it?

Charles Yes.

Lady Marchmain I don't understand it. I simply don't understand how anyone could be so callously wicked. I'm not going to reproach you. Any failure in my children is my failure. But ... I don't understand how you could have been so nice in so many ways, and then do something so wantonly cruel. I don't understand ... how we all liked you so much. Did you hate us all the time? I don't understand how we deserved it. No, I don't understand ...

Charles stands, not knowing what to say. Music. The Marchmain family are all looking at Charles. This is held for a beat or two, then Charles turns and walks away

The Lights cross-fade following Charles's move across the stage. He sets up his easel, which establishes his Paris studio

SCENE 3

Charles's Paris studio

Charles paints during Cordelia's reading of the letter and Julia's telephone call

A single spot comes up on Cordelia

Cordelia Darling Charles, I was so very miserable when you went. You might have come and said goodbye! I hope you're happy in Paris. I am in disgrace too. I sneaked whisky for Sebastian and got caught. He did seem to want it so. And there was (and is) an awful row. Mr Samgrass has gone (good!) — I think he's in disgrace, too. Mr Mottram is very popular with Julia (bad!) and is taking Sebastian away (bad! bad!) to a German doctor. Julia's tortoise disappeared. We think it buried itself, as they do, so there goes a packet (expression of Mr Mottram's). I am very well; with love from Cordelia.

The spot fades on her while another comes up on Julia on the other side of the stage

Julia Hallo. Charles? I'm so sorry to bother you like this, but it's Mother. She really wants to see you. Look, I can't explain on the telephone. Could you come? I can't speak for long, now. Do think about it, Charles. I'd be really grateful. ...Yes. ... Thank you, Charles. Goodbye.

The spot fades on Julia

Rex (*off*) Charles! Charles!

Rex enters

There you are. I came this morning, but you were out. I've been looking
all over Paris. Have you got him?

Charles You must mean Sebastian.

Rex Yes.

Charles Has he given you the slip, too?

Rex Damned nuisance! We were going on to the clinic in Zurich today. I
went round to the Travellers for a game of cards last night, had a run of luck,
and cleaned up a packet. And do you know Sebastian must have pinched
the lot while I was asleep. It's a bit much, going off like that. I was rather
hoping that if I made a good job of him, it might do me a bit of good in
another direction. You're not hiding him by any chance?

Charles No. My dealings with that family are over. At least I thought they
were ...

Rex She piled it on a bit thick at your last meeting, did she not?

Charles "Callously wicked" ... "wantonly cruel" ...

Rex I'll tell you a thing, Charles, that Ma Marchmain hasn't let on to anyone.
She's a very sick woman. You know, she really might peg out any minute.

Charles Ah, I see ...

Rex What?

Charles Julia's telephone call, this morning.

Rex Was she trying to trace me?

Charles No. She said her mother wanted to see me. I'm leaving tomorrow.

Rex Yes, well things may well have taken a turn for the worse. But I'll tell
you another thing — they'll get a jolt financially if they don't look out.

Charles I thought they were enormously rich.

Rex Well, they are; but they just let their money sit quiet. I don't mean they'll
be paupers; the old boy will always be good for the odd thirty thousand a
year, but I'll tell you, I'd like to get the little matter of a marriage settlement
through, before the shake-up comes. Trouble is, it's far from straight-
forward — there's religion, for a start. I've bent over backwards to make
things easy — I've said Julia can go to church whenever she wants to. I like
a girl to have religion. I've even said that she can bring the children up
Catholic. Like I said to Ma Marchmain, "Just give me the form, and I'll sign
on the dotted line." I can't understand it — you'd think they'd be all over
themselves to have me in, but they're forever putting obstacles in the way!
I mean, they must know I can be a lot of help to them one way and another!

But then there's my past ... you may know I've been tied up with someone else for a year or two.

Charles Mrs Champion? (*He begins to remove his artist's smock and puts on a jacket*)

Rex Yes. Well that's all washed up. Julia doesn't care anyway. And I don't see how it's anyone else's business. But to cap it all, we have what Julia calls "Bridey's Bombshell".

Charles What was that?

Rex He found out that I was married before. In Montreal.

Charles Ah ...

Rex I explained that I was divorced. But to Catholics the word divorce appears to have no meaning. So, anyway, I'm off to Venice. See if I can square old Marchmain — I gather he's likely to agree to anything that'll upset Lady M. But first I'd better do my best to find Sebastian. (*At the door*) Give me the wink if you stumble across him, will you?

He exits

Charles turns and walks into the next scene. The Lights cross-fade

SCENE 4

Brideshead

Julia It's sweet of you to come. Mummy has been asking for you, but I don't know if she'll be able to see you now after all.

Charles Is she very ill?

Julia Yes. She's dying. She may live a week or two, or she may go at any minute. She's asleep now, but I can tell you what she wanted to say ... she was beastly to you, last time you met. She knows now that she was wrong about you ... she wanted to apologize.

Charles There's no need.

Julia I was so sorry when you had to go. You'd become such a part of us ... But there's another thing. Sebastian — she wants him. I don't know if that's possible, is it?

Charles I hear he's in a very bad way ... I met with Blanche in London. After he'd given Rex the slip, Sebastian stayed with him in Marseille, I gather — he was out of funds, stealing from his host, pawning what he took, and drinking the proceeds! A sot is how Blanche described him. Last heard of living in Fez with a German out of the Foreign Legion ...

Julia Oh, Charles! (*She touches his arm*) It seems as if everything is changing, and nothing can stop it. Will you try and get him? I think Sebastian would want it, too, if he realized.

Charles I'll try.
Julia Thank you. Thank you so much. There's ... no-one else I could ask ...

She exits

Charles turns, and the Lights cross-fade

SCENE 5

Sebastian's house in Fez

Kurt enters on crutches

Charles I'm looking for Sebastian Flyte. This is his house, is it not?
Kurt Yes. But he isn't up yet.
Charles I've come from England to see him on important business. Does he
   normally lie in bed at this time?
Kurt He has not been well. The brothers took him away to the infirmary at
   the top of the hill. They looked after him. The Franciscans are good fellows.
   I got to go there myself one day soon to have my foot dressed. You're not
   Sebastian's brother?
Charles I'm only a friend. We were at university together.
Kurt I had a friend at the university. We said, "What the hell? There is no
   work in Germany. Germany is down the drain", so we said goodbye to our
   professors, and they said, "Yes, Germany is down the drain. There is
   nothing for a student to do here now." So we joined the Legion. My friend
   died of dysentery last year. When he was dead, I said "What the hell?", so
   I shot my foot. It is now full of pus, though I have done it a year.
Charles Really? Well now, my immediate concern is with Sebastian.
Kurt He is very good fellow, Sebastian. He brought me here. Nice house,
   nice food, nice servant — everything is all right for me here, I reckon. And
   he looks after me. I like it here all right.
Charles His mother is very ill. I have come to tell him.
Kurt She rich? His mother rich?
Charles Yes.
Kurt Then why don't she give him more money? Then we could live at
   Casablanca, maybe, in a nice flat. You know her well? You could make her
   give him more money?
Charles What's the matter with him?
Kurt I don't know. I reckon maybe he drink too much.

Sebastian comes to the doorway

Sebastian Charles! What are you doing here?
Charles I've come looking for you. How are you?
Sebastian I'm fine, now. But I was out of my mind for a day or two. Kept thinking I was back in Oxford. Well, Charles, this is a surprise!

There is an awkward moment when Charles wonders if he should deliver his message, then Kurt starts to limp towards the door

Kurt I must go dress my foot.

Sebastian helps him to the door

Sebastian I'll come through in a minute. (*He watches him into the next room*) Steady, now. (*He turns back to Charles*) Kurt's been lost without me. I've been in hospital.
Charles Yes, I know.
Sebastian I won't ask you if you like him; no-one does. It's funny: I couldn't get on without him, you know. But ... why have you come?
Charles It's your mother. She's really ill. Dying, I'm afraid. She really wanted to see you before ... but I can see that's going to be impossible. When you're better ... will you consider going back to England?
Sebastian It would be lovely in some ways; but do you think Kurt would like it?
Charles For God's sake, you don't mean to spend all your time with Kurt, do you?
Sebastian I'm happy, he's happy.
Charles Happy?
Sebastian You see, Charles, it's rather a pleasant change when all your life you've had people looking after you, to have someone to look after yourself. Only, of course, it has to be someone pretty hopeless to need looking after by me.
Charles Kurt tells me your money isn't getting through.
Sebastian Oh, it's the lawyers again.
Charles I'll see your bank manager. He can hold your allowance and pay you weekly from it. And a reserve for emergencies, when he's convinced you really need it. Would that suit?
Sebastian Thanks. Yes. Otherwise Kurt will get me to sign for the whole lot when I'm tight, and then he'll go off and get into all kinds of trouble.
Charles Well, you obviously can't travel back yet.
Sebastian No. (*Slight pause*) Is Mummy really dying?
Charles It's taken so long for me to find you, she's ... probably dead by now. The doctors only gave her a few days.

Sebastian Poor Mummy. I don't believe she had a friend in the world. Poor, poor Mummy.
Kurt (*off; calling*) Sebastian!
Sebastian (*calling*) Just coming! (*To Charles*) I'll have to see to him. His foot's pretty bad ... Is there ... anything else?
Charles No. Nothing else.
Sebastian (*going to him*) Don't be cross with me, Charles. We were such good friends, once.
Charles Yes. Yes, we were.

There is a moment when a parting embrace is possible; then:

Kurt (*off*) Sebastian!
Sebastian Goodbye, Charles. Do look after yourself.

He exits

Music. In the original production, this link included a solemn funeral mime, using Lady Marchmain's empty chair as a focus. Charles turns, and walks downstage, picking up his easel as he does so and placing it so that he is looking out over the audience as he begins to paint

SCENE 6

Marchmain House, London

Cordelia enters

Cordelia May I stay here and watch?
Charles I don't mind. I shan't do much more today.
Cordelia When will it be finished?
Charles Tomorrow, I expect.
Cordelia You've seen Sebastian? He won't come home, even now?
Charles No.
Cordelia It's good of you to paint Marchmain House for us. It's been our London home for so long. Nothing like as nice as Brideshead, of course, but it's such a shame it's coming down. They're putting up a block of flats, you know. Mummy would have hated it; at least she was spared that. Rex wanted to take what he called a penthouse at the top. Isn't it like him? Poor Julia. Everything seems in such a muddle now.
Charles What's going to happen to you?
Cordelia What, indeed? There are all kinds of suggestions. Rex and Julia talk of taking over half Brideshead and living there. Papa won't come back. We

thought he might, but no ... they've closed the chapel. Mummy's requiem was the last mass said there. After she was buried, the priest came in — I was there alone, I don't think he saw me — and took out the altar stone and put it in his bag; then he burned the wads of wool with the holy oil on them and threw the ash outside; he emptied the holy-water stoup and blew out the lamp in the sanctuary, and left the tabernacle open and empty, as though from now on it was always to be Good Friday. I suppose none of this makes sense to you, Charles, poor agnostic. I stayed there till he was gone, and then, suddenly, there wasn't any chapel there anymore, just an oddly decorated room.

Charles Well, there was a time before when it was just a part of the house — it's simply returned to that. It's gone. Just as Sebastian has gone, and Julia has gone.

Cordelia Ah, but God won't let them go for long. Do you remember the Father Brown story Mother read us, the night Sebastian first got drunk? Father Brown said something like, "I caught the thief with an unseen hook and an invisible line which is long enough to let him wander to the ends of the world and still to bring him back with a twitch upon the thread."

Charles You know, although I stayed with you, and talked with her many times, I never really knew your mother.

Cordelia You didn't like her. I think when people wanted to hate God they hated Mummy.

Charles What?

Cordelia She was saintly, but she wasn't a saint. No-one could hate a saint, could they? They can't hate God, either. When they want to hate him and his saints they have to find something like themselves and pretend it's God and hate that. I suppose you think that's all bosh.

Charles I really don't know ...

Cordelia I hope I've got a vocation.

Charles Vocation?

Cordelia It means you can be a nun. If you have vocation, you can't get away from it.

Charles (*smiling at her*) I expect you'll fall in love.

Cordelia Oh, pray not ...! But what will happen to you?

Charles Well, I'm engaged, did you know?

Cordelia Yes. To Celia.

Charles You approve?

Cordelia I think she's very suitable. Rather attractive ... very interested in your work.

Charles So you think I've made a good choice?

Cordelia Oh, yes. A sound investment, I'd say.

Charles What do you mean?

Cordelia Oh ... nothing. And then a career as an architectural painter, is that it?

Charles You make it sound so dull!

Cordelia I didn't mean to. I think you have a great talent.

Charles (*stopping painting and looking at her*) But ...

Cordelia What?

Charles There's a "but", I can hear it!

Cordelia (*looking at the picture*) Well, don't you ever get the urge to paint something really outlandish? If I could paint, I'd use the most sensational colours imaginable!

Charles And you want to be a nun?

Cordelia Of course. We each have our vocation. We can't escape from it.

Charles (*shaking his head*) One day I hope to understand your family.

Cordelia One day you will. (*She starts to go*)

Brideshead enters

Morning, Bridey.

Brideshead I hope you haven't been disturbing Charles.

Cordelia We've just been having a little talk. Thank you for letting me watch. Bye.

Cordelia exits

Charles Cheerio.

Brideshead (*coming to look at painting*) It's very good.

Charles Thank you. I think that'll do for today. (*He begins to pack up his things*)

Brideshead Charles ... do you consider that there is anything vicious in my brother's connection with this German?

Charles No. I'm sure not. It's simply a case of two waifs coming together.

Brideshead But isn't he a criminal?

Charles Only to the military. He was dishonourably discharged.

Brideshead And the doctor says Sebastian is killing himself with drink?

Charles Weakening himself — he hasn't d.t.'s or cirrhosis.

Brideshead He's not insane?

Charles Certainly not. He's found a companion he happens to like, and a place where he likes living.

Brideshead Then he must have his allowance as you suggest. The thing is quite clear ... you know, when the flats are built they're going to keep the name — Marchmain House. We can't stop them, apparently.

Charles What a sad thing.

Brideshead Well, I'm sorry it's coming down, of course. But do you think it's good architecturally?

Charles One of the most beautiful houses I know.

Brideshead Is it really? I've always thought it rather ugly. But there you are: you artists ... see things that I don't. At least I can understand your paintings, they're not ...

Charles Outlandish?

Brideshead Of course not! One can see quite clearly what they are.

Charles (*starting to move off with his materials*) Hmmm ... Perhaps Cordelia was right.

Brideshead Why? What did she say?

Charles Oh, it doesn't matter. (*He starts to go*)

Brideshead I'm afraid she talks nonsense almost the whole time.

Charles (*stopping, then turning and smiling*) I'm not so sure about that.

Charles exits

Julia (*off*) Bridey! Bridey! Are you there?

Brideshead Julia?

Julia enters

Julia Oh, out here. Has Charles finished?

Brideshead Yes. He's just gone.

Julia I've been taking a last look round. All the rooms are so bare, so cold. And next week all this will be rubble. It's awful, isn't it?

Brideshead I suppose it is awful, in a way. But I'm afraid I've never been able to see it as more than a place to stay when the family were in London.

Julia I think it's a marvellous house.

Brideshead Yes? Hmmm ... Charles thinks so, too.

Julia He's done a wonderful job with the paintings, don't you think? Captured the house for ever. (*Slight pause*) What do you think of his marriage, Bridey?

Brideshead What? What should I think of it?

Julia Well ... has he made the right choice, do you think?

Brideshead I'm not sure I'm qualified to say, but yes, I think so; after all, Celia is a good business-woman. In many ways it's an obvious partnership.

Julia But do you think they'll be happy?

Brideshead Why shouldn't they be?

Julia I ... don't know. I suppose they'll make the best of it.

Brideshead What?

Julia Could you possibly give me a lift, Bridey?

Brideshead Why? Has Rex gone without you?

Julia Yes ... he's ... terribly busy at the moment, you know how it is.
Brideshead Well, all right. But you'll have to come now. I've got to lock up
  and deliver the key to the solicitors.
Julia (*starting to go*) You can drop me off there. I'm ... meeting someone.
  (*She stops at the door*) I'm glad you think Charles will be all right.

*She smiles at Brideshead and exits. He looks after her for a moment, then
also exits*

SCENE 7

Charles enters

*South American music begins; a short, lively dance in which brightly
coloured cloths are woven across the stage and around Charles; then the
cloths are unwound from him and we hear a ship's hooter*

The Lights change to represent an ocean liner

*We see passengers disembarking and coming aboard, meeting and parting.
Charles exits*

Celia enters and sees Julia, who enters across the stage

Celia (*calling*) Julia! Julia!
Julia (*surprised*) Celia!
Celia Well I never! Fancy meeting up like this!
Julia Yes, extraordinary! I never expected to see you here, Celia. Have you
  been visiting New York, too?
Celia Not really, I'm meeting Charles. We're sailing back together.
Julia Oh ... yes ... I seem to remember reading in the paper something about
  his going away — a painting trip, wasn't it?
Celia Yes. That's it. Rather a long one — it's been nearly two years.
Julia Two years! Celia! What's he been doing?
Celia Looking for ... inspiration. He's done some rather good exotic stuff,
  actually — it was sent on ahead, so I've had a good look. Quite a change
  in style: very exciting, full of colour.
Julia Where has he been?
Celia Mexico, Central America — old palaces, derelict churches, weird and
  wonderful vegetation ... I think they're going to sell very well.
Julia But didn't you want to be with him?
Celia Oh! I couldn't. Not with the children, you see.

Julia Children? I thought you only had the one — John, isn't it?

Celia We have a daughter now. She was born soon after Charles went away. I'll tell you what — we'll have a little party, shall we? There are several friends on board. I'll send you an invitation.

Julia Thank you. It would be nice to see Charles again.

She sees Charles "coming aboard" behind Celia's back

Well, if you'll excuse me, I've got a couple of things I must see to. We'll no doubt meet up later.

She exits

Celia Yes! Bye ... (*She turns to see Charles*)

Their eyes meet, and they slowly walk towards each other. A cool embrace

(*After a pause*) It's been a long time.

Charles Yes. But you might have come along.

Celia Oh, Charles. It was never going to be suitable for the children. I couldn't have given birth to Caroline in the jungle!

Charles Why did you call her that?

Celia After Charles, of course.

Charles Ah ...

Celia Now that Johnjohn has a companion ——

Charles Who?

Celia Your son, darling.

Charles For Christ's sake, why do you call him that?

Celia It's the name he invented for himself. He talks of you such a lot. He prays every night for your safe return. Do you know, I don't believe you've changed at all, Charles.

Charles No, I'm afraid not.

Celia Do you want to change?

Charles It's the only evidence of life.

Celia But you might change so you didn't love me anymore.

Charles There is that risk.

Celia Charles. You haven't stopped loving me?

Charles You said yourself that I hadn't changed.

Celia Well, I'm beginning to think you have. I haven't.

Charles No ... no, I can see that.

Celia Were you at all frightened at meeting me again?

Charles Not the least.

Celia You didn't wonder if I should have fallen in love with someone else in the meantime?

Charles No. Have you?

Celia You know I haven't. Have you?

Charles No ... no. I'm not in love.

Celia Looking forward to getting home? I've got a surprise for you.

Charles Yes?

Celia I've turned the old barn into a studio so you needn't be disturbed by the children, or when we have people to stay.

Charles I rather liked that barn.

Celia But you'll be able to work there, won't you? There's a lot of work waiting. I promised Lady Anchorage you would do Anchorage House as soon as you got back. That's coming down, too — shops and flats. You don't think that all this colourful work you've been doing is going to spoil you for that sort of thing?

Charles Why should it? It's just another jungle closing in.

Celia Good. We can start again exactly where we left off. It's going to be a lovely trip. I thought we'd have a cocktail party this evening. There's such a lot of friends on board — did you know Julia was here? I haven't seen her for years.

Charles Nor have I. Have you found our cabin?

Celia It's only just up there. Number six. I must go and see the steward about the food.

She exits. Julia enters

Charles Julia!

Julia Hallo, Charles.

Charles How are you?

Julia I'm ... well. And you?

Charles Yes, I'm fine.

Julia Celia told me you were coming on board. It's strange ... meeting like this. I can't remember the last time ... must be ages. I never seem to see anyone I like. I don't know why.

Charles What have you been doing in America?

Julia Don't you know?

Charles No.

Julia I'll tell you about it sometime. I've been a mug. I thought I was in love with someone, but it didn't turn out that way. I long to see the paintings you've been doing on your trip ...

Charles You may find them disappointing.

Julia I'm sure I won't. (*Pause*) I can't remember when we last met, can you? All those years ...

Charles Yes ...
Julia It's hard to picture you as the pretty boy Sebastian brought home with him.
Charles Have I aged terribly?
Julia No. No. It's not that. You look ... lean and grim. Harder, too.
Charles And you're softer.
Julia Yes, I think so ... and very patient now.
Charles Sadder, too.
Julia Oh yes. Much sadder ...
Charles Shall we ... walk for a bit?

They start to walk

Tell me about Rex.
Julia Rex? Must I?
Charles I suppose I mean, "Tell me about you."
Julia Oh, well ...
Charles It's been such a long time. So much must have happened.
Julia No. Nothing has happened. Nothing that matters.
Charles Why New York?
Julia Escape, I suppose. Looking for something that doesn't ever seem to be there.
Charles Yes, I know ...
Julia It was a rather silly liaison that seemed as though it might be important for a while, then ...
Charles And you and Rex?
Julia Dead. Over.
Charles Has he left you?
Julia No. Not left me ... it's just finished. We're ... out of love ...
Charles Have you children?
Julia Oh, Rex so wanted a child — his child. But I needed an operation. Well, eventually, he persuaded me ... and I conceived ... but it was born dead.
Charles I'm sorry. How did Rex take it?
Julia Rex? I sometimes think he has no real feelings ... he's just ... a few faculties of a man, highly developed; the rest simply isn't there. Do you know, he couldn't imagine why it hurt me to find two months after we came back to London from our honeymoon, that he was still keeping up with Brenda Champion?
Charles I was glad when I found Celia was unfaithful. I felt it was all right for me to dislike her.
Julia Do you? I'm glad. I don't like her, either. Why did you marry her?
Charles Physical attraction, ambition — everyone agrees she's the ideal wife for a painter. And probably loneliness, missing Sebastian ...

Julia You loved him, didn't you?
Charles Oh yes. He was the forerunner ...

Julia has stopped walking

Is this your cabin?
Julia Yes. (*She goes in*)

He follows her

(*After a pause*) Do you know, last year, when I thought I was going to have a child, I'd decided to have it brought up a Catholic? I thought, "That's the one thing I can give her. It doesn't seem to have done me much good, but my child shall have it." But I couldn't even give her life ...
Charles What made you think of that?
Julia Sebastian ... you ... all the things mixed together — Death, Judgement, Heaven, Hell, Nanny Hawkins and the catechism. All together, all part of oneself. All part of a plan. Perhaps that's why you and I are together like this?

Charles goes to kiss her. She stops him

I don't know. I don't know if I want love.
Charles Love? I'm not looking for love.
Julia Oh yes, Charles, you are.

He holds her

Charles Well ... perhaps I am. What are your plans?
Julia London for a bit. What about you ... and Celia?
Charles Oh, I think Celia's going straight home. She wants to see the children.
Julia Will you go?
Charles No.

They look at each other — the final recognition of love

No. I'm not going.

She eases free from his hold and turns away

Julia Good. (*She begins to slip the top of her dress down*)

Charles (*softly*) Now?
Julia (*turning to him*) Yes. Now.

They embrace. The Lights cross-fade to:

SCENE 8

Music. Lights. We see a board that says: "Private View: Ryder's Latin America"

There is a dance/movement sequence which depicts critics and public admiring Charles's work. The dance is punctuated by cries of "Amazing!", "Wonderful!", "So different", "Exquisite!", and so on. The group dance off, their comments fading as they do so

Celia and Charles enter

Celia It's gone extraordinarily well, you know.
Charles Has it?
Celia The comments, darling! They love it—one of the critics said he'd seen it coming years ago.
Charles What?
Celia All this. The new style. You're going to be very busy. Lots of commissions. Plenty of room in the new studio, of course. Now, when we get home, we must ——
Charles Celia ...
Celia What? (*She looks at him*) What is it?
Charles I have to tell you now. I'm not coming home.
Celia Not coming home? What do you mean?
Charles I'm not coming home today with you. I'm ... I'm going down to Brideshead this evening.
Celia Charles! No! Not tonight, Charles; you can't go there tonight! You're expected at home. You promised, as soon as the exhibition was done, you'd come home. Johnjohn and Nanny have made a banner with "Welcome" on it. And you haven't seen Caroline yet.
Charles (*after a pause*) I'm sorry. It's all settled.
Celia You haven't seen the new studio. You can't go tonight. You haven't ... Was it ... Julia who asked you down?
Charles Yes.
Celia Did she ask me?
Charles I knew you wouldn't be able to come.
Celia Well, I can't now. I could have if you'd have let me know earlier.
Charles Sorry.

There is a pause while they look at each other, taking stock

Celia I'd better go, then ... it's been a terrific success, hasn't it? I'll ... think of something to tell them at home ... (*Pause*) Charles ...
Charles Yes?
Celia I ... I wish it hadn't got to happen quite this way ...

She exits. Blanche enters, talking to someone off stage

Blanche No, I have not brought a card of invitation. I don't want my photograph in the *Tatler* — I came to see the pictures! Now I shall explain them to the artist! (*He turns and holds out his hand to Charles*) Charles!
Charles Antoine!
Blanche My dear, there's a gorgon through there who thinks I am gate-crashing! I only arrived in London yesterday, and heard quite by chance at luncheon that you were having an exhibition, so of course I dashed impetuously to the shrine to pay homage. You see, I've been watching you, my dear. I'm a faithful old body. I went to your first exhibition. I found it — charming. Not quite my cup of tea. Too English, you see. But then I heard that you had gone to the tropics, became a Gauguin. I was all agog! But what have I found here? Lots of colour, yes — but no substance! A very naughty and very successful practical joke! Charm! Creamy English charm!
Charles You're quite right ...
Blanche My dear, of course I'm right! Don't you remember all those years ago when I warned you about charm? It kills love; it kills art. Well I'm sorry ... but there you are.
Charles Thank you. I wish there were no truth in what you say, but I know how right you are. I'm afraid I have to catch a train, Antoine, otherwise I'm sure you'd set me straight. I really appreciate your coming.
Blanche A loving gesture, freely given, as always. May I ask where you are off to?
Charles Brideshead.
Blanche Ah yes ... of course. You are going to be charmed to death ... Farewell ...

He exits

SCENE 9

Music. The Lights change. The mood changes as we arrive once more at Brideshead

Julia is seated. Charles walks slowly towards her

Charles My darling! I saw you through the window. Is anything wrong? You
seemed to be sitting so still out here.
Julia No, nothing's wrong. I was just thinking, just remembering ...
Charles What?
Julia Everything, really. But especially how we met ... quite by chance.
Charles On the liner?
Julia Yes ... The oddest coincidence ... or perhaps not.
Charles A very lucky coincidence, I'd say. (*He kisses her*)
Julia How many days have there been since then, when we haven't seen each
other? A hundred, do you think?
Charles Not so many.
Julia We've had ... what? ... more than two years. How many more, Charles?
Charles A lifetime.
Julia I want to marry you.
Charles Of course. When the divorces are done.
Julia There'll be war. This year, next year ... I want a day or two with you
of real peace.
Charles Isn't this peace? Julia ... what do you mean by "peace", if not this?
Julia So much more ... sometimes I feel the past and the future pressing so
hard on either side that there's no room for the present at all!

They embrace each other

Brideshead enters

They move apart, half guiltily

Bridey! I wasn't expecting you.
Brideshead Well, well — only you two. I hoped to find Rex here.
Julia You'll just have to make do with us. What's the news?
Brideshead As a matter of fact, I have some news ... you know, if I was Rex
I'd want to live here in my constituency.
Julia Rex says it saves four days' work a week not to.
Brideshead I'm sorry he's not here. I have a little announcement to make.
Julia Bridey, don't be so mysterious. Out with it.
Brideshead Well ... I am engaged to be married. I hope you are pleased.
Julia Bridey! How very exciting. Who to?
Brideshead Oh, no-one you know. She is called Mrs Muspratt; her Christian
name is Beryl.

Julia laughs

A widow. Why do you laugh?

Julia I'm sorry. It's just so unexpected. Where did you find her?

Brideshead Her late husband, Admiral Muspratt, collected matchboxes.

Julia You're not marrying her for her matchboxes?

Brideshead No ... no ... I had a letter from Papa this morning giving me his approval. He has been urging me to marry for some time.

Charles Congratulations.

Brideshead Thank you.

Charles Have you brought her with you?

Brideshead Oh, I couldn't do that, you know.

Julia Why not? I'm dying to meet her. Let's ring her up now and invite her. She'll think us most peculiar leaving her at home alone at a time like this.

Brideshead She has the children. Besides, you *are* peculiar.

Julia What?

Brideshead It wouldn't be suitable. After all, I am a lodger here. This is Rex's house at the moment, so far as it's anybody's. What goes on here is his business. But I couldn't bring Beryl here.

Julia But ... why?

Brideshead Beryl is a strict Catholic. It is a matter of indifference to me whether you choose to live in sin with Rex or Charles or both — I have always avoided inquiry into the details of your ménage — but Beryl could never consent to be your guest.

Julia Why, you pompous ass ... (*She goes to one side*)

Charles Bridey, what a bloody offensive thing to say to Julia.

Brideshead There was nothing she could object to. I was merely stating a fact well-known to her.

Brideshead exits

Charles goes to Julia. She is crying

Charles My darling, you mustn't mind. It doesn't matter what that old booby says.

Julia It's ... just the shock. Don't laugh at me ...

Charles The cold-blooded old humbug.

Julia No. It's not that. He's quite right.

Charles What do you mean?

Julia "Living in sin". He's right. Not just ... doing wrong, as I did when I went to America. No. That's not what it means.

Charles Julia ——

Julia Just sin. One flat deadly word that covers a lifetime. It's my idiot child, this sin that I have reared, nursed and guarded from the world. And now it's grown so strong, it can devour its mother.

Charles No, Julia.

Julia Yes! All the past, all the future, is within its reach. This sin ... Christ
dying with it, nailed hand and foot, hanging at noon high above the crowds
and the soldiers. Hanging forever ... never the cool sepulchre, never the oil
and spices in the dark cave. My little sin, nameless and dead, like the baby
they wrapped up and took away before I had seen her ... (*She breaks down*)
Charles Julia ... Julia ...

He comforts her. She calms down

Julia Well ... Bridey is the one for bombshells, isn't he? I'm sorry for all that.
Charles That's all right. It's just that ... I'm in there, somewhere, involved
with what you call your sin, and yet I can't understand.
Julia And I can't explain. Charles — am I going crazy?
Charles Of course not. But I can't believe that all that came from just a few
words of Bridey's! You know at heart that it's all bosh, don't you?
Julia How I wish it was. All I can hope to do is to put my life in some sort
of order. That's why I want to marry you. I should like to have a child.
That's one thing I can do ...

SCENE 10

Mr Ryder's house

Music. The Lights cross-fade to a spot on Charles's father

Mr Ryder So you're being divorced? Isn't that rather unnecessary, after
you've been happy together all these years? I distinctly remember seeing
you together — last Christmas, was it, or the one before? — and thinking
how happy you looked, and wondering why. You'll find it very disturbing,
you know, starting off again. How old are you — thirty-four? That's no age
to be starting again. I do call re-marrying a lot of nonsense. I can understand
a man wishing he hadn't married and trying to get out of it, but to get rid
of one wife and take up with another immediately is beyond all reason.
Take my advice, my dear boy, and give up the whole idea.

The Lights cross-fade to:

SCENE 11

Brideshead

Julia enters

Julia Charles! What do you think? My father. He's decided to come home, to Brideshead.
Charles When?
Julia Soon. He's decided to spend his last years here.
Charles Oh dear!
Julia What?
Charles Poor old Bridey. Just when he and his plain and simple Beryl were going to take over Brideshead!
Julia Yes. Mrs Muspratt's been full of it for weeks: from workaday housewife to mistress of a great house! She's going to be hard hit. But look who else has come home!

Cordelia enters

Cordelia Charles! How lovely to see you again!
Charles Cordelia. You've changed! Where have you been? Spain, wasn't it?
Cordelia Yes. Helping in the prison camps. But ... I've seen Sebastian!
Charles What, in Spain?
Cordelia No, Tunis. He's with the monks there. I wanted him to come home with me, but he wouldn't. He's got a beard now, and he's very religious. The Superior said he just turned up one day and asked to be admitted as a lay brother, but he didn't want to do the training, so he was sent away. He kept coming back, drunk, several times a week, until one day they found him lying unconscious outside the main gate. They put him in the infirmary — he was very ill — and he's been in and out of there ever since.
Charles How dreadful. But does he ... I mean, is he suffering?
Cordelia Oh yes. But that will help him — it's the spring of love, you see.
Charles Oh, now ——
Cordelia I know you don't understand. You understand so little. Poor Cordelia, you think; grown up a plain and pious spinster, full of good and rather foolish thoughts. Isn't that what you think?
Charles Well ... I don't know.
Cordelia You see, Sebastian is nearer to God now than ever. One morning, after one of his drinking bouts, he'll be picked up at the gate dying, and show by a mere flicker of an eyelid that he is conscious when they give him the last sacraments.
Charles Perhaps I'll never understand.
Cordelia Oh, the snow on the mountain moves slowly. But it does move.
Cordelia
Julia } *(together as if in a catechism)* Just a little sun will do it.

Scene 12

Music

Lord Marchmain enters upstage, walking with great pain, supported by Cara

Charles, Julia, and Cordelia turn to them

Lord Marchmain I daresay I shall not be really fit again until summer comes. I look to you four to amuse me. I'd like to know ... the circumstances of Brideshead's courtship. It puzzles me. He and his wife dined with me in Rome ... since we are all members of the family I can speak without reserve. I found her deplorable ... How my son, with a very free choice among the women of England can have settled on — I suppose I must call her so — Beryl, I really can't imagine. I am appalled at the prospect of — of Beryl taking what was once my mother's place in this house. I don't think she would be quite in her proper element here, do you? Who shall I leave it to? Sebastian, alas, is out of the question. Who wants it? Would you like it, Cara? No, of course you would not. Cordelia? I think I shall leave it to Julia and Charles.

Julia Of course not, Papa. It's Bridey's!

Lord Marchmain And ... Beryl's? I will have Gregson down one day soon and go over the matter. It's time I brought my will up to date ... I have rather a fancy for the idea of installing Julia here ... but what do they say in England about the war? I suppose you no longer have access to political information, Julia?

Julia I think it is generally assumed that it is inevitable.

Lord Marchmain Really? In Italy they think otherwise — that it will all be "arranged". But you. (*He turns to Charles*) You will no doubt become an official artist?

Charles No. As a matter of fact I am negotiating now for a commission in the Special Reserve.

Lord Marchmain Oh, but you should be an artist. I had one with my squadron during the last war, for weeks — until we went up to the line. Well ... I'll sleep now.

Cara starts to help him off

Julia Good-night, Father.
Charles Good-night.
Cordelia Night.

Cara kisses him and he exits

Cara (*turning to the others*) Yes. He has come home to die. The doctors in Rome gave him very little time.

Julia What is it?

Cara His heart; some long word of the heart. He is dying of a long word.

She puts her arm around Cordelia and exits with her

Charles Do you think he really means to leave it to us?

Julia Yes, I think he does.

Charles But it's monstrous for Bridey.

Julia Is it? I don't think he cares much for the place. I do, you know. He and Beryl would be much more content in some little house somewhere.

Charles You mean to accept it?

Julia Certainly. It's Papa's to leave as he likes. I think you and I could be very happy here ...

SCENE 13

Solemn music. The Lights slowly fade to a dim gloom

Cara and Cordelia bring Lord Marchmain on in a bath chair. He is near death

Brideshead enters, looks closely at his father, then turns to Julia and Charles

Brideshead Papa must see a priest. I'll get Father Phipps.

He exits

Charles Julia! Are they going to let the priest in here? Can't they even let him die in peace?

Julia They mean something so different by "peace".

Charles But it would be an outrage! No-one could have made it clearer, all his life, what he thought of religion. They'll come now, when his mind's wandering and he hasn't the strength to resist, and claim him as a death-bed penitent. It's all superstition and trickery. Don't you agree?

Julia I don't know, Charles.

Charles How can we stop this tomfoolery?

Julia Why should we?

Charles You know as well as I do. It's ... unseemly.

Julia Who am I to object to unseemly incidents? Anyway, what harm can it do? I asked the doctor about it, actually — I knew it was bound to happen. He said it could act as a stimulant, or it might alarm him ——

Charles Well, there you are!

Julia Charles, I really can't see why you should take it so much to heart that
my father shall not have the last sacraments. What are you fighting?

Charles It's such a lot of witchcraft and hypocrisy.

Julia Is it? Anyway, it's been going on for nearly two thousand years. I don't
know why you should suddenly get in a rage now. For Christ's sake, write
to *The Times*, get up and make a speech in Hyde Park, start a "No Popery"
riot, but don't bore me about it. What's it got to do with you or me whether
Father sees his parish priest?

Lord Marchmain Better today. Better today. We live long in our family and
marry late. Seventy-three is no great age.

Cordelia enters

I have lived carefully, sheltered myself from the cold winds ... slept in my
own sheets ... I shall live long ... if only I could breathe ... when the summer
comes ... I shall leave my bed and sit in the open air and breathe more easily.
What became of the chapel?

Cordelia They locked it up, Papa. When Mummy died.

Lord Marchmain It was her special place. I gave it to her ... then I went
away. I left her in the chapel, praying. I never came back to disturb her
prayers. They said we were fighting for freedom ... I had my own victory.
Was it a crime? Cordelia? Was it a crime?

Cordelia I think it was, Papa.

Lord Marchmain Is that why they've locked me in this cave, do you think?
But the wind will come soon, tomorrow perhaps, and we'll breathe again.
Better tomorrow.

Julia (*to Cara*) Is it the end?

Cara Yes; he's very near, I think.

Brideshead enters with Father Phipps

Charles You're going ahead with this, even though you know the shock may
kill him? Cara? What do you think?

Cara I don't want him made unhappy. That is all there is to hope for now;
that he'll die without knowing it. But I should like the priest here, all the
same.

Charles (*standing in the priest's path*) Father, you know Lord Marchmain
has not been a practising member of your church for twenty-five years?

Father Phipps Oh. I am well aware of that, my son.

Charles Do you honestly believe ... do you really think it's possible that he
can change now, after all that time of unbelief?

Father Phipps Thank God, by His grace it is possible. I have seen so many men and women die. I never knew them sorry to have me there at the end.

Charles But they were Catholics. Lord Marchmain has never been one except in name, for marriage purposes. He was a scoffer. Cara said so.

Father Phipps Christ came to call not the righteous but sinners to repentance.

Lord Marchmain groans

Julia Father. Please don't delay.

She looks at Charles. This is the moment they know their relationship is at an end

I take full responsibility for whatever happens. Will you please see my father now?

Soft music begins. Father Phipps goes to Lord Marchmain and bends over him. Charles stands apart

Father Phipps Now ... I know you are sorry for all the sins of your life, aren't you? Make a sign, if you are. You're sorry, aren't you? Try and remember your sins. Tell God you are sorry. I am going to give you absolution. While I am giving it, tell God you are sorry you have offended him ... (*He takes out a little silver box of oils and anoints Lord Marchmain. Then he softly intones the final blessing*)

Charles (*turning to the audience*) Oh God, if there is a God, forgive him his sins, if there is such a thing as sin.

He turns to look as Lord Marchmain pulls himself up a little, and weakly makes the sign of the cross, before sinking back. Brideshead, Cordelia, Cara and Julia kneel and cross themselves. The music ends. They all stand

Lord Marchmain is wheeled off by Cara. Brideshead, the Priest, and Cordelia follow

Julia walks towards Charles

Charles (*taking her by the hand*) Little to say ...

Julia Yes ... you know, don't you?

Charles Since this morning. Since before this morning. All this year ...

Julia I didn't know until today. Oh, my dear, if you could only understand.

Then I could bear to part, or bear it better. I ... can't marry you, Charles; I can't be with you ever again.

Charles I know. What will you do?

Julia Just go on — alone. Probably I'll be bad again, punished again. But the worse I am, the more I need God. I can't shut myself out from His mercy. That is what it would mean, starting a life with you, without Him. (*She begins to cry*) It ... it may be a private bargain between me and God, that if I give up this one thing I want so much, however bad I am, he won't quite despair of me in the end ... Now we shall both be alone, and I shall have no way of making you understand.

Charles I don't want to make it easier for you — I hope your heart may break ... but I do understand ... I do understand ...

Music. The Lights fade

Julia turns and walks slowly away from Charles. Charles exits

SCENE 14

The grounds at Brideshead. 1943

When the Lights come up again the music fades

We see Hooper enter, studying the papers on his clipboard. Then he looks up

Hooper Well, I'm blowed! There's even more stuff over here, by the chapel, and it's not even on my list. Someone's made a right mess of things. Every time we move it's the same problem. It wouldn't do in business, I can tell you. If the Army was a business, it'd be bankrupt in a month, the way they run things. Oh, the CO says we're to clear up the house for Brigade. Did you hear? Ryder?

Charles enters. He has put on his army greatcoat and cap once more

Charles What?

Hooper We've got to clear the rooms up. CO asked me to tell you. Fatigue party of fifty. Wants you to have a good look round inside the house first and report to him on the damage. (*He looks again at his papers*) Oh, this is hopeless. I'll have to get HQ's copy of this lot. Nothing matches up.

Charles Oh ... right. I'll take that look around, then.

Hooper Right-ho. Hope there's not too much mess. I'll come and find you.

Hooper exits

As he does so, we see Nanny Hawkins emerging from the chapel. She genuflects, then turns and almost bumps into Charles

Charles Nanny Hawkins.

She looks at him

Do you know who I am?
Nanny It's ... it's Mr Ryder.
Charles How are you, Nanny?
Nanny Well, this is a surprise ... a uniform, is it?
Charles Yes. I've been billeted here.
Nanny Oh. Oh, I see. What a surprise!
Charles I had no idea until we arrived.
Nanny There's no-one here, you know. The military turned them out.
Charles Oh ... what about Julia ... and Cordelia?
Nanny Gone to the war, the two of them together. Did you hear Mr Mottram on the wireless last night? Very nasty he was about Hitler. I said to the girl Florence, who does for me, "If Hitler was listening, and if he understands English, which I doubt, he must feel very small!" Who would have thought of Mr Mottram doing so well?
Charles Where is Julia?
Nanny Cordelia wrote only last week. They're together still, and they're both very well, though they couldn't say where, but Father Phipps said, reading between the lines, it was Palestine, which is where Bridey's Yeomanry is, so that's very nice for them all! But it is good to see you again, Mr Ryder.
Charles It's good to be here, Nanny. But I'm afraid I'll have to get on, got a job to do.
Nanny All right, dear.
Charles I'll come and see you, if that's all right?
Nanny Oh, come as often as you like. Yes, do. It'll be nice to have you part of us again. (*She starts to exit, then stops and turns*) Cordelia always said you'd come back, but I didn't think you would ...

She exits

Charles watches her go, then turns. Music begins, as when Sebastian and Charles first entered the chapel. Charles walks slowly into the chapel and stands still for a second or two, bows his head slightly, as if in prayer, and then crosses himself. Hooper comes purposefully in, but stops when he sees Charles

Hooper Oh, sorry. I didn't realize ——
Charles (*turning*) What?
Hooper I wondered where you'd got to. I didn't know you were ... er ...
Charles It doesn't matter. I was just checking things were all right in here.
Hooper Have you had a look round? What's the situation?
Charles Fine. Yes, it's fine. (*He looks thoughtfully out over the audience*)
Hooper What's up, Ryder? Something on your mind?
Charles I was thinking about the lamp. The light that's shone for two
thousand years ... there's hope in that, don't you think?
Hooper Depends what you believe, I suppose.
Charles Does it? (*Thoughtfully positive*) Yes, perhaps it does ...
Hooper We'd better make our report, then ... (*He starts to go out, then turns
to Charles*) We can tell 'em not too much damage done, can we?
Charles (*smiling*) Yes, I think we can say that. Not too much damage, after
all.

*The music swells and the Lights slowly fade on Charles, who is smiling,
radiant and happy*

CURTAIN

FURNITURE AND PROPERTY LIST

ACT I
SCENE 1

On stage:	Nil
Off stage:	Clipboard (**Charles**) Clipboard (**Hooper**) Torch (**Hooper**)

SCENE 2

On stage:	Nil

SCENE 3

On stage:	Nil
Personal:	**Sebastian:** Aloysius, visiting card

SCENE 4

On stage:	Chair with Aloysius Megaphone

SCENE 5

On stage:	Green cloth

SCENE 6

On stage:	Nil
Personal:	**Nanny:** rosary

SCENE 7

On stage:	Nil
Off stage:	Wet copy of *Antic Hay* (**Blanche**) Books (**Charles**)

Sketchpad (**Charles**)
2 towels (**Blanche**)
Coat (**Blanche**)

Personal: **Sebastian:** Aloysius

SCENE 8

On stage: Nil

Off stage: Book containing telegram (**Mr Ryder**)
Overcoat (**Charles**)

SCENE 9

On stage: Nil

Off stage: Bath chair (**Sebastian**)

SCENE 10

On stage: Chair
Easel
Drawing supplies
Aloysius

SCENE 11

On stage: Bottle of wine
2 glasses
2 small bags

SCENE 12

On stage: Nil

SCENE 13

On stage: 2 chairs
Book for **Charles**

Off stage: Bottle (**Sebastian**)
Bottle (**Rex**)

Personal: **Sebastian:** Aloysius

Scene 14

On stage: Nil

Personal: **Mulcaster:** money
               Charles: money
               Sebastian: money

Scene 15

On stage: Embroidery hoop with needle and thread for **Lady Marchmain**

Off stage: Bottle of whisky (**Sebastian**)

Scene 16

On stage: Chair
               Aloysius

ACT II
Scene 1

On stage: Clipboard
               Bottle
               Chairs
               Photographs

Personal: **Charles:** wallet containing one-pound note, five-pound note

Scene 2

On stage: Nil

Off stage: Box (**Julia**)
               Easel (**Charles**)

Scene 3

On stage: No props required

Scene 4

On stage: Nil

Scene 5

On stage: Nil

Off stage:	Chair Easel (**Charles**)
Personal:	**Kurt:** crutches

Scene 6

On stage:	No props required

Scene 7

On stage:	No props required

Scene 8

On stage:	A board reading "Private View: Ryder's Latin America"

Scene 9

On stage:	Chair

Scene 10

On stage:	Nil

Scene 11

On stage:	Nil

Scene 12

On stage:	Nil

Scene 13

On stage:	Nil
Off stage:	Bath chair (**Lord Marchmain**) Silver box of oils (**Father Phipps**)

Scene 14

On stage:	Nil
Off stage:	Clipboard and papers (**Hooper**)

LIGHTING PLOT

Interior and exterior settings.
No practical fittings required.

ACT I, Scene 1

To open: Bring down house lights; sweep spots to simulate lorry headlamps.
Bring up final light on **Charles** and light behind gauze on **Flytes**

Cue 1   **Charles** smiles   (Page 1)
Fade light behind gauze; bring up dawn effect

Cue 2   **Charles:** "... it must be ... twenty years ..."   (Page 3)
Fade on **Hooper**; *bring up light behind gauze on* **Mr Ryder**

ACT I, Scene 2

To open: Bring up interior lighting

No cues

ACT I, Scene 3

To open: Bring up night effect

No cues

ACT I, Scene 4

To open: Day effect

No cues

ACT I, Scene 5

To open: Summer afternoon effect

No cues

ACT I, Scene 6

To open: Interior effect, with spot on **Nanny**

Cue 3   **Sebastian** and **Charles** come out of the room   (Page 11)
              Fade spot on **Nanny**

Cue 4   **Sebastian:** "You must see that."   (Page 11)
              Change to chapel effect

ACT I, Scene 7

To open: Interior effect

No cues

ACT I, Scene 8

To open: Ryder house effect

No cues

ACT I, Scene 9

To open: Brideshead effect

No cues

ACT I, Scene 10

To open: Outdoor effect

No cues

ACT I, Scene 11

To open: Bright sunshine effect

No cues

ACT I, Scene 12

To open: Venice effect

No cues

ACT I, Scene 13

To open: Oxford effect

No cues

ACT I, Scene 14

Cue 14   All exit after the **Policeman**   (Page 35)
              Cross-fade to Brideshead effect

ACT I, Scene 15

Cue 15   **Sebastian** exits   (Page 39)
              Fade

Cue 16   **Sebastian** flops into a chair   (Page 39)
              Bring up daytime interior effect

ACT I, Scene 16

Cue 17   **Charles** and **Sebastian** hold each other tightly   (Page 40)
              Fade

ACT I, Scene 17

To open: Bring up Ryder house effect   (Page 40)

Cue 18   **Charles** turns to look at **Aloysius**   (Page 41)
              Fade to spot on **Aloysius**; *hold, then cut to black-out*

ACT II, Scene 1

To open: Bring up light on **Charles** and light behind gauze on **Flytes**;
              when ready, change to Brideshead effect

Cue 19   **Sebastian** and **Charles** look at each other   (Page 45)
              Cross-fade to hunting sequence effect

ACT II, Scene 2

Cue 20   **Sebastian** rides away from the others   (Page 46)
              Change back to Brideshead effect

Cue 21   **Charles** walks away   (Page 49)
            Cross-fade to studio effect

ACT II, Scene 3

To open: Bring up spot on **Cordelia**

Cue 22   **Cordelia:** "... love from Cordelia."   (Page 49)
            Fade spot; bring up spot on **Julia**

Cue 23   **Julia:** "Thank you, Charles. Goodbye."   (Page 49)
            Fade spot

Cue 24   **Charles** turns and walks across the stage   (Page 51)
            Cross-fade to Brideshead setting

ACT II, Scene 4

Cue 25   **Julia** exits. **Charles** turns   (Page 52)
            Cross-fade to **Sebastian's** *house in Fez*

ACT II, Scene 5

Cue 26   **Sebastian** exits   (Page 54)
            Change to funereal lighting; when ready, cross-fade
            to interior effect

ACT II, Scene 6

No cues

ACT II, Scene 7

To open: General bright lighting; when ready, change to exterior effect

Cue 27   **Julia** and **Charles** embrace   (Page 63)
            Cross-fade to art exhibition lighting

ACT II, Scene 8

No cues

ACT II, SCENE 9

To open: Change to exterior lighting for Brideshead effect

No cues

ACT II, SCENE 10

To open: Cross-fade to a spot on **Mr Ryder**

Cue 28   **Mr Ryder:** "... give up the whole idea."   (Page 67)
              Cross-fade to Brideshead effect

ACT II, SCENE 11

No cues

ACT II, SCENE 12

No cues

ACT II, SCENE 13

To open: Fade to a dim gloom

Cue 29   **Charles:** "I do understand ..." 2nd time   (Page 73)
              Fade to black-out

ACT II, SCENE 14

To open: Bring up exterior effect

Cue 30   **Charles:** "... after all."   (Page 75)
              Slow fade to black-out

EFFECTS PLOT

ACT I

Cue 1	To open *Music. Sound of lorries passing*	(Page 1)
Cue 2	**Hooper:** "Brideshead." *Music*	(Page 2)
Cue 3	**Charles:** "... I know all about it ..." *Music*	(Page 3)
Cue 4	To open Scene 3 *Music*	(Page 4)
Cue 5	**Charles** begins reading *A bell tolls*	(Page 4)
Cue 6	To open Scene 4 *Music*	(Page 5)
Cue 7	**Sebastian:** "We'll get you for that!" *Music*	(Page 7)
Cue 8	**Blanche** exits *A clock chimes*	(Page 7)
Cue 9	**Sebastian** and **Charles** exit *Music*	(Page 8)
Cue 10	**Sebastian** and **Charles** exit *Music*	(Page 9)
Cue 11	**Sebastian:** "You must see that." *Organ music*	(Page 11)
Cue 12	**Sebastian:** "It was Papa's present to Mama." *Fade organ music*	(Page 12)

Cue 13	To open Scene 7 *Students chanting, cheering and laughing as per text p. 12*	(Page 13)
Cue 14	**Charles** and **Sebastian** hop and wheel round the room *Music*	(Page 21)
Cue 15	To open Scene 12 *Music*	(Page 28)
Cue 16	To open Scene 13 *Music; wind and Oxford bells tolling*	(Page 30)
Cue 17	**Sebastian:** "It might be fun ..." *Music*	(Page 32)
Cue 18	**Mulcaster** and the **Policeman** struggle *A car starts and crashes*	(Page 35)
Cue 19	**Policeman:** "Come on, sir." *Music*	(Page 35)
Cue 20	**Sebastian** exits *Clock chimes*	(Page 39)
Cue 21	**Charles:** "*Contra mundum*, Sebastian!" *Soft music; fade to begin next scene*	(Page 40)
Cue 22	**Charles:** "Sebastian! Sebastian!" *Music swells*	(Page 41)

ACT II

Cue 23	To open *Music*	(Page 42)
Cue 24	To open Scene 2 *Music*	(Page 46)
Cue 25	**Sebastian** exits *Funereal music*	(Page 54)
Cue 26	**Charles** enters *South American music; a ship's hooter*	(Page 58)

Cue 27	**Julia** and **Charles** embrace *Music*	(Page 62)
Cue 28	To open Scene 9 *Music*	(Page 63)
Cue 29	To open Scene 10 *Music*	(Page 67)
Cue 30	To open Scene 12 *Music*	(Page 69)
Cue 31	To open Scene 13 *Solemn music*	(Page 70)
Cue 32	**Julia:** "... see my father now?" *Soft music; continue until* **Lord Marchmain** *dies*	(Page 72)
Cue 33	**Charles:** "I do understand ..." 2nd time *Music; fade to open Scene 14*	(Page 73)
Cue 34	**Charles** turns *Organ music, as for Cue 11*	(Page 74)
Cue 35	**Charles:** "... after all." *Music swells*	(Page 75)

Milton Keynes UK
Ingram Content Group UK Ltd.
UKHW021855080124
435668UK00038B/673